NEW DIRECTIONS FOR CHILD DEVELOPMENT

William Damon, *Brown University*
EDITOR-IN-CHIEF

Creativity from Childhood Through Adulthood: The Developmental Issues

Mark A. Runco
California State University, Fullerton

EDITOR

Number 72, Summer 1996

JOSSEY-BASS PUBLISHERS
San Francisco

CREATIVITY FROM CHILDHOOD THROUGH ADULTHOOD:
THE DEVELOPMENTAL ISSUES
Mark A. Runco (ed.)
New Directions for Child Development, no. 72
William Damon, Editor-in-Chief

Microfilm copies of issues and articles are available in 16mm and 35mm,
as well as microfiche in 105mm, through University Microfilms Inc., 300
North Zeeb Road, Ann Arbor, Michigan 48106-1346.

ISSN 0195-2269   ISBN 0-7879-9871-0

NEW DIRECTIONS FOR CHILD DEVELOPMENT is part of The Jossey-Bass
Education Series and is published quarterly by Jossey-Bass Inc., Publishers,
350 Sansome Street, San Francisco, California 94104-1342. Second-class
postage paid at San Francisco, California, and at additional mailing
offices. POSTMASTER: Send address changes to New Directions for Child
Development, Jossey-Bass Inc., Publishers, 350 Sansome Street, San Francisco, California 94104-1342.

SUBSCRIPTIONS for 1996 cost $59.00 for individuals and $87.00 for institutions, agencies, and libraries.

EDITORIAL CORRESPONDENCE should be sent to the Editor-in-Chief,
William Damon, Department of Education, Box 1938, Brown University,
Providence, Rhode Island 02912.

Cover photograph by Wernher Krutein/PHOTOVAULT © 1990.

TCF Manufactured in the United States of America on Lyons Falls
Pathfinder Tradebook. This paper is acid-free and 100 percent
totally chlorine-free.

CONTENTS

EDITOR'S NOTES

The chapters in this issue of *New Directions for Child Development* each focus on development and creativity. Why development and creativity? One reason is that developmental issues cut across many other topics in studies of creativity. The biological underpinnings of creativity, for example, probably exert their influence in different ways at different points in development, and the cognitive and emotional mechanisms of creative thinking vary in different chronological stages. Even more obvious are the educational implications of developmental theories of creativity. I will go so far as to propose that we must understand the development of creativity or we will not really understand creativity.

Each chapter in this volume is based on a presentation given at a meeting of the American Psychological Association. All but one were given as part of the "Development and Creativity" symposium at the 1995 meeting in New York City. The exception is the chapter from Ruth Richards, which is an adapted version of her presentation from the 1994 meeting in Los Angeles. The chapters are being published in the order in which they were originally given in the symposium, with the chapter from Ruth Richards published last. With her concerns about societal values and creativity as variability, her chapter may have the widest applicability and as such is a good way to end. (What you see listed as the last chapter in the Table of Contents is really just my list of recommended readings on the topic of development and creativity.)

The order of chapters has a chronological basis, at least in the sense that each contributor emphasizes the creativity of a particular period of development. Sandra Russ and I each emphasize the potentials of children; Robert Albert describes several important developmental changes during adolescence; and Robert Keegan presents the view that the creativity of adults is "different in degree" from that of youth. Richards has quite a bit to say about children, but her point about creativity and variability applies throughout the life span.

Each contributor to this volume is well aware of development occurring across the life span. Keegan, for example, discusses the role played by knowledge in the creativity of adults—knowledge that children have not yet developed—but he does recognize the potentials of children. Differences of opinion among the chapters in this volume, such as they are, are reflected in emphases rather than mutually exclusive claims about development.

This is not to say that everyone agrees about creativity and development. I can use my chapter as an example because I suggest that in several important ways children are more creative than older individuals. After all, they make fewer assumptions and are open to wider possibilities, and they are less concerned about altering their ideas for some sort of presentation or recognition. In this volume and elsewhere in the research literature you will see what is essentially the diametric view, namely that children are not truly creative. In this view, children do not try to be creative and may in fact be original only because they do not know any better. They lack the strategies, intentions, and knowledge that adults employ in their creative efforts. The point is that there are debates in this area and described in this volume. This makes for good reading, and reading with practical importance. "Practical importance" may suggest reading for parents and teachers, but it is much grander than that. Creativity is an integral part of development, and our understanding of creativity thus contributes significantly to our understanding of our continued personal and societal development.

Mark A. Runco
Editor

MARK A. RUNCO is professor of child development at California State University, Fullerton, president-elect of the Psychology and the Arts Division of the American Psychological Association, and editor of the Creativity Research Journal.

Creativity is defined so as to allow for both continuities and discontinuities in development.

Personal Creativity:
Definition and Developmental Issues

Mark A. Runco

Creative behavior often seems to be childlike. Indeed, there is a famous statement from Picasso in which he claims to have become a good painter only after he learned to see like a child, and Gardner (1994) recently suggested that eminent creators are childlike in their behavior and thinking. Barron (1995) described how "innocence to experience runs the human course. And, with luck, back to innocence again. *To see things as though for the first time is a mark of the artist.* Organized innocence. Innocence-in-experience. Something saved from the shock of growing up. Something given back in the artist's work."

Innocence is indicative of youth or perhaps naïveté, and in fact Abra (1989) tied creativity specifically to naïveté. Henri Matisse reportedly claimed that "you study, you learn, but you guard the original naïveté" (quoted in Charlton, 1994, p. 34). Does all this mean that creativity is a result of a kind of atypical development in which aspects of immaturity are retained? One thesis in the present article is that creativity is not entirely childlike, and in fact for the most part creative thinking is only childlike in a metaphorical way.

The primary objective of this chapter is to present a definition of creativity that recognizes both developmental continuities and discontinuities. This definition is predicated on the idea that creativity requires a special combination of skills; some of these reflect maturity and experience and some reflect behaviors that are found in early childhood. The combination of maturity and immaturity—and continuity and discontinuity—is possible because creativity is multifaceted; it is a *complex* or *syndrome* and relies on a variety of traits, skills,

I would like to express my gratitude to Stephanie Dudek, Howard Gruber, Lloyd Noppe, and Laurisa Shavinina for comments on an early draft of this article.

3

and capacities (Albert and Runco, 1989; MacKinnon, 1960; Mumford and Gustafson, 1988). It is thus possible for some of the traits and skills to mature while others remain relatively stable. The assumption of multidimensionality is necessary for the definition of *creativity as manifested in the intentions and motivation to transform the objective world into original interpretations, coupled with the ability to decide when this is useful and when it is not.*

This chapter reviews the evidence for the various parts of that definition—in particular, transformational capacity, discretion, and intentionality. This requires some discussion of metaphoric logic, the construction of interpretations, values, knowledge, strategy, and choice. All of these topics except transformational capacity have been reviewed before, so for all but that one I will merely summarize the earlier conclusions and cite exemplary research. Most of my attention here is devoted to transformational capacities, the underlying mechanism for controlled interpretations, and to developmental issues.

Transformation and Interpretation

Individuals familiar with the creativity literature may be surprised that transformational abilities are emphasized in the definition above, rather than some more commonly cited thinking style or process, such as the ability to find original or remote associates (Eysenck, in press; Mednick, 1962). Transformational capacities are emphasized because they are so general, and because they underlie the creative thinking of individuals of all ages.

A transformation occurs whenever we interpret the objective world (that is, make sense of sensory information). Even very young children transform their experiences, and in fact they do so in an uninhibited, playful, and original fashion. Granted, transformations are not always original and useful—they are not always creative. That is where discretion comes in. More will be suggested about that later in this chapter.

Piaget (1976a) gave great weight to transformations. He even suggested, "Believe me, thinking cannot be reduced to speaking, to classifying objects into categories, nor even to abstracting. To think is to act on the object and to transform it" (p. 90). This supports my idea about transformation being a fundamental aspect of information processing and creativity. All nonreflexive information processing requires an interpretation of some sort, and all interpretations are dependent on the individual's treatment of the available information.

Piaget (1976a, 1976b) further described *adaptation* as a kind of assimilation and accommodation, the former referring to changes made so that informational input will fit with existing cognitive structures, and the latter referring to changes in structures in response to new information. Piaget argued that subjective experience is a personal construction, but that is just another way of saying that it is interpretive and thus idiosyncratic. Subjective experience and objective experience are far from isomorphic.

Though on a general level Piaget's view of transformation as a means for modifying information is compatible with the definition of creativity presented here, his findings about children should not be taken to suggest a lower age limit for creative thought. I am referring to his view that certain transformations would not be expected until the concrete operational stage. Adaptation and personal constructions are apparent much earlier, and the assimilation involved relies on a kind of transformation. Moreover, the transformations Piaget manipulated in his experiments on conservation and the like were *logical transformations,* and creativity need not be logical, at least in the conventional sense. It relies on the individual's own personal logic, with personal criteria for the usefulness and originality of a solution and a personal interpretation of whether or not some experience is problematic. When thinking creatively, the individual may explore hypothetical possibilities, and these are not necessarily logically possible, as might be implied by Piagetian theory. They are instead feasible irrespective of standard or formal and objective logic. It is formal logic that comes to constrain divergent thinking as children grow; if logical hypothetical skills were necessary for personal transformations we would of course not see these before formal operations. Evidence for the capacity for transformations at a very young age (two to three years) was presented by Kavanaugh and Harris (1994), and of course there is a large body of research on pretending, which is a good indicator of uninhibited interpretations (Singer and Singer, 1990).

Transformations contribute to more than just the solving of problems; they also play a role in the identification and definition of problems. Root-Bernstein (1993) was aware of this when he divided "transformational thinking" into the translation of a problem into "some internalized fantasy of a visual, kinesthetic, tactile or combined sensual form" and a change of an insight into an expression, typically verbal, mathematical, or another shared symbol system. Root-Bernstein used the term *synscientia* to describe successful transformational thinking. This was derived from synesthesia and scientia (to know).

Transformations are also no doubt involved when an individual becomes so immersed in a project that the self is lost; often creative individuals report that they somehow become one with the problem. Barron (1995) described this as a merger of self and nonself, or subject with object. Not surprisingly, he also emphasized the ego strength that would help transformations by supplying the confidence required to invest so much time in working to transform and innovate. Ego strength will allow the individual to stand up to pressures to conform, and this may be vital because interpretive transformations are by definition personal, at least initially, and therefore can be rather unconventional. Clearly, this applies most directly to adults: conventions may have little impact during childhood (Rosenblatt and Winner, 1988; Runco and Charles, in press; Wolf and Larson, 1981) and confidence and ego strength may thus be superfluous until egocentricism is outgrown. Courage would only be necessary for the child if and when he or she explores personally (rather than socially) uncomfortable ideas (see Dudek and Verreault, 1989; Russ, 1988).

Sternberg and Lubart (in press) suggest that "creative people are well able to transit between conventional and unconventional thinking. They find the transition relatively comfortable, and do it with ease. Less creative people, in contrast, even though they may have the facility to exercise with ease and even speed an array of more routine mental processes, find it difficult to transit between conventional and unconventional thinking." Sternberg and Lubart base their conclusions on work with novel concepts, but the idea of a *transit to unconventionality* fits nicely with Barron's (1995) idea of a merger of self and nonself. It is also consistent with research on unconventionality and creativity (for example, Eisenman, 1992; Runco, 1993a).

Maslow (1971) also tied creativity to a blurring of object and self. In his words, being "lost in the present . . . seems to be the sine qua non for creativeness of any kind" (p. 60). He further described creative work as a "loss of self or ego . . . transcendence . . . fusion with the reality being observed" (p. 62). There is, for Maslow, a total fascination of the matter in hand, "giving up the past," "giving up the future," "an innocence in perceiving and behaving." Not surprisingly, Maslow's view is entirely compatible with that presented in this chapter, and this includes his recognition of the creativity of children. He noted how children are generally free of expectations and "children are more able to be receptive in this undemanding way" (p. 64).

Transformational capacities thus underlie the construction of personal interpretations. (Incidentally, for shorthand I refer to the definition of creativity presented herein, with discretionary and intentional transformations, as the *interpretive definition.*) These interpretations are personal; they may not be social. The assumption is that creativity does not require outward expression. Impact and reputation are often tied to creativity (for example, in Kasof, 1995), as is the expressiveness of children (Dudek, 1974; Rosenblatt and Winner, 1988), but for the sake of parsimony, and to the degree that my definition and its emphasis on subjective interpretations is useful, the social aspects of creative work should be kept separate from the personal (Runco, 1995). This also has a developmental justification because transformational abilities may develop before the individual is prepared for (or motivated to) socially significant work. Recall here the premise of a complex or syndrome and the idea that the facets within the syndrome may mature at different rates.

Why do individuals transform their experiences? One reason reflects a motivation to innovate. Abra (in press), for example, argues that "Creativity immediately brings to mind the great achievers of art and science. . . . but in fact this phenomenon . . . can be found in virtually every human endeavor ranging from football to flower arranging. It is responsible for everything called progress, for every step we have taken away from a primitive animal existence. Because of its machinations, our environments are now almost entirely artificial, shot through with products that come about because someone got a bright idea." Innovation is a process of altering, of adapting—in a word, a process of transformation. It is often external, in contrast to the personal transformations suggested earlier, but then again personal changes may be most important when they lead to external changes, that is, to innovations (see Rickards and De Cock, in press).

This brings up several issues that are critical for a definition of creativity. One follows from the distinction between creativity and innovation, and from the role of adaptation in each. Innovation is often seen as adaptive, which makes great sense because it is largely external—a product is altered and presumably improved. This was demonstrated very clearly by Weber (in press) and his review of the invention of the chair. Weber suggested that this kind of transformation "involves starting with a known product and then applying formal operations to it to generate a candidate new entity which may be useful . . . transformations can yield qualitative differences in function . . . for example, stretching and flattening transformations applied to a chair we sit on will generate an elongated form like a couch." The controversial part of this may follow from the common idea that creativity is a kind of adaptation (Cohen, 1989; Flach, 1990; March, 1987). Adaptation is in some ways a kind of reaction: if it is truly a *re*action, it may be too dependent on the situation at hand to be truly original. Runco and Sakamoto (1996) put it this way: "There is a paradox about adaptability. The paradox is that [adaptation] might lead . . . to uncreative activity and behavior. If the environment does not require originality, the most adaptable individuals will fit in by being unoriginal." Runco and Sakamoto concluded that adaptation may require some moderate (rather than extreme) creativity, and that reinforces the part of my definition that posits that creative individuals learn to transform, but they do so *only some of the time*. They rely on their discretion, in addition to their transformational capacities.

The parallel developmental question is whether or not children's egocentricism keeps them from considering external opportunities for innovation. Very young children seem to focus on the here-and-now, and although all children explore very frequently in their play, this is much more process- than product-oriented. It is the exploration itself that motivates rather than the outcome. Evidence for such ambivalence about innovating was given by empirical research on the environmental cues used by children (see Runco and Charles, in press).

Just as creativity can be distinguished from adaptation, so too can it be distinguished from problem solving. This was implied earlier in the discussion of problem identification and definition (also see Runco, 1994b), but it is also supported by the theory that some kinds of creativity reflect self-expression. In this light, creativity is not dependent on problems. This is, for instance, suggested by views of creativity as self-actualization (Maslow, 1971; Runco, Ebersole, and Mraz, 1991), and by the recent work of Heinzen (1994) on the need for proactive (rather than reactive) creativity in organizations.

The distinctiveness of creativity from problem solving may be clarified by the fact that problems are themselves interpretations. Schuldburg (1994, p. 98) quoted Wittgenstein in this regard, the latter having written in the early 1960s about "the disappearance of problems," which is a nice description of how obstacles can be challenging rather than problematic. Schuldberg himself called it a dissolving of previously insoluble personal, technical, or aesthetic problems. Surely most of us have had the experience of perceiving a problem, only to think more about it and be challenged by it so much so that it is no longer problematic. It is *transformed* into a challenge, and therefore not undesirable. Once immersed in it, the individual loses that outside perspective and in a very real sense becomes one with the problem. This is what was meant by a blurring of self and nonself. It may also be intimated by the empathy of creative persons (Root-Bernstein, 1993, p. 19; Wakefield, 1994). They may empathize with their work and problem.

What is most important here is the idea that the problematic nature of certain experiences is dependent on one's interpretation: one individual might find a situation problematic, while a second individual finds the same situation an enjoyable challenge. This may sound like two labels for the same thing, but consider the subsequent emotions. The first individual may very well feel anxiety while the second feels nothing but pleasurable anticipation.

Returning to the question about motivation, creative persons might transform experience into original interpretations in an effort to innovate. What else motivates them to transform? Very likely, many transformations are motivated by cognitive preferences. There is, for example, a general and possibly lifelong interest in novelty (Berlyne, 1960), and innovation can supply new stimuli and maintain diversity of opportunity. Such novelty may in turn be desirable because it maintains arousal (Martindale, 1990). On preferences, I can quote Porter and Suefeld (1981) and their theory that complex integrative and conceptual processing "is open and flexible. New interpretations of the same event may be made and considered simultaneously, and more complex rules are used to interrelate the perspectives. Individuals exhibit high information seeking and tolerance for uncertainty" (p. 322). Their use of interpretations is compatible with my own, and the idea of seeking uncertainty fits with what I said about individuals using what they know.

Because transformations have their own kind of logic, individuals probably put energy into them as a way of using what they know. In that sense, it is a matter of cognitive efficiency, or what Hofstadter (1985) called the mind's "path of least resistance." Whatever the descriptor, an interest in "using what you know" would help explain why certain individuals are drawn into particular fields, and why talented individuals often report a fit between their temperaments and their chosen career (Albert, 1990).

Something more can be said about the logic used to transform experience. I have suggested that it is a logic that is unique to creative thinking. Levine (1984) called it *metaphoric logic* and suggested that it "permits recognizing isomorphic structures between entities which from the 'common sense' viewpoint appear to be quite different" (p. 90). Metaphoric logic can explain why children often appear to be *cognitive aliens* (Elkind, 1979), and why their play, art, language, and behavior is so often unconventional and surprising. Research on children's art, for example, suggests that their most creative work ignores conventions (Rosenblatt and Winner, 1988). Similarly, there is evidence from the linguistic domain that indicates that children are most creative before the fourth grade (Gardner, 1982; Torrance, 1968). In the fourth grade there is a slump, probably because of increased conformity and conventionality. No doubt children learn that they can fit best into society if they rely on particular perceptual and intellectual tendencies, if they rely on standard logic and symbols. Unfortunately, those tendencies tend to reflect a kind of routine or even fixity. This is readily apparent in the maturational process Gardner (1982) used to explain the predisposition for a literal stage of development, during which figurative and original thinking are at their lowest.

The *metaphoric* label for this kind of logic is an especially apt one given that metaphor use is so often related to creative insight (Clement, 1988; Gibbs, in press; Gruber, 1988; Khatena and Khatena, 1990; Rothenberg and Hausman, in press) and given the possibility that what I have called "transformations" will often result in a metaphorical insight or expression. Data supporting this were presented by Clement (1988). He administered the "spring problem" to scientists and found that most analogical solutions reflected a kind of transformation rather than some associative operation. Clement proposed that this kind of transformation is not deductive nor inductive, and he argued that it is used in the solving of a wide range of scientific problems. This conclusion in turn supports Rothenberg's (in press) and Davis, Keegan, and Gruber's (in press) work with eminently creative scientists.

Other support for the existence of a distinct and nonrational conceptual system was given by Epstein, Lipson, Holstein, and Huh (1992). They described two conceptual systems, one representing experiential processes and the other representing rational processes. They specifically argued that "each [is] operating by its own rules of inference" (p. 328). One system may be rational in a conventional sense, and the other rational only in what I am calling a metaphorical sense. Recall here what was proposed earlier in this chapter about the limitations of Piagetian theory for our understanding of the kinds of transformations that apply to creative thinking.

The connection between metaphors and transformations reinforces what was proposed about the universality of the latter. Indeed, Gibbs (in press) described metaphors as "fundamental to human thought. It is near impossible for us to conceive of ourselves, others, and the world we live in without embracing the power of metaphor. We use metaphor not only to linguistically express our thoughts, but to make sense of our everyday experiences and to establish coherence out of an inchoate world" (p. 198). The universality of metaphors and transformations is still further supported by data showing that individuals use metaphors four or five times each minute, or approximately once every twenty-five words (see Gibbs, in press).

Other research has been conducted on transformations, some of which does not focus on metaphors or the like. Guilford (1983), for instance, emphasized transformations in his last publication about creativity. He suggested that "from an exploratory study . . . it could be concluded that transformation abilities are more important than divergent-production abilities in creative thinking" (p. 75). The exploratory study relied on rankings given by scientists to structure-of-intellect factors. Subotnik (1988) obtained similar results in her research on the ratings given by gifted adolescents.

Taylor (1964), O'Quin and Besemer (1989), and Puccio, Treffinger, and Talbot (1995) used a criterion that was defined in terms of transformations (for example, reformulation) in research with judges rating potentially creative products. There might be a concern because this line of work relies on evaluations of products, and hence the underlying interpretive processes can only be inferred. In addition to requiring inferences about thinking, this emphasis may put children at a disadvantage because they may not be so concerned with outcomes and products, even when they think creatively (Dudek, 1974; Runco and Charles, in press).

Feldman, Marrinan, and Hartfeldt (1972) took a slightly different approach, and one that might not put children at a disadvantage. This is because they obtained ratings of ideas elicited by divergent thinking tests, which are often used with children (Runco, 1992). Feldman, Marrinan, and Hartfeldt defined *transformational power* as "the extent to which a given response represents the production of new forms rather than improves upon existing forms, the extent to which the apparent constraints of the stimulus situation are overcome, but overcome in a highly appropriate fashion, and the extent to which the product generates additional thoughts in the observer" (p. 336). Feldman, Marrinan, and Hartfeldt found that about one in every eight original ideas was also characterized by its transformational power. Like the research on products (for example, Taylor, 1964), this investigation relied on subjective judgments of transformational power, but agreement among judges was relatively high (80 percent). Incidentally, this investigation was essentially an empirical test of the prediction given by Jackson and Messick (1967) about criteria for creativity. They too recognized the importance of transformational power.

Guilford (1983) himself collected original data representing ten "basic transformation abilities," five of which are symbolic and five semantic. He found these ten factors to be obliquely related, but also found two higher-order transformation factors, one for the symbolic tests and one for the semantic, in addition to one third-order factor. Guilford described a list of tests of transformational capacities (for example, "seeing confused words," "daffynitions," "memory for misspellings," and "camouflaged words"). These might be used in future research (see Khattab, Michael, and Hocevar, 1982).

After a recent reanalysis of some of Guilford's data, Bachelor and Michael (1991) concurred about the significance of transformations and about the fit of both first- and higher-order factors for the SOI (structure of intellect) model. They argued that

> Of particular psychological importance to the study of creativity was the empirical demonstration . . . of two factors not associated with divergent production—namely sensitivity to problems and redefinition. . . . Redefinition, or flexibility

of closure, constitutes the convergent production of figural, semantic, or symbolic transformations. . . . In the instance of semantic material, one would be
given a familiar object . . . and then be required to generate new information to
be used for a unique and single purpose or for the attainment of a specific objective in an almost totally unfamiliar or strange context (as in using a guitar string
to slice a piece of cake or cheese in the absence of a knife).

Other research suggests directions for new research on transformations
and creative interpretations. One possibility would be to adapt methods cur-
rently being used to study *counterfactual thinking,* which has been defined as
"the construction and use of alternatives to reality" (Boniger, Gleicher, and
Strathman, in press). This is much like pretending, which Harris (1994) saw
when "the child will often put aside reality" (p. 19).

Some of my own empirical work is intended to facilitate the transformation of problems. These studies present different kinds of explicit instructions
to subjects, some containing conceptual or declarative information, and some
procedural and strategic. Of most relevance are the instructions that present
subjects with strategies for restructuring the problem at hand. I am interested
in the different kinds of instructions and varying the levels of explicitness, so
some manipulations might be quite literal (for example, "turn it [the problem]
on its head") while others are themselves metaphorical (for example, "dig
deeper" or "make the familiar strange"). Based on earlier research with explicit
instructions (reviewed in Runco, 1994b), my colleagues and I expect to find
significant individual differences in the degree to which subjects can utilize the
different kinds of instructions, and differences in the degree to which they
actually transform the given information. We typically rely on divergent thinking tasks in this work, but parallel work is being conducted by Reiter-Palmon,
Mumford, Boes, and Runco (1995) with other kinds of ill-defined problems,
and by Martinsen (1995) with insight problems. Other quantitative efforts
might utilize Barron's Symbolic Equivalence Test (see Barron, 1995).

Qualitative research would also be informative, especially if it sampled
artists. Jones (1995) did just this and uncovered numerous examples of how
professional artists transform their experiences into their work. Dudek (in
press) wrote "the final artistic composition is therefore the result of unsolicited,
urgently felt decisions made at the level of primary process and the intentional
decisions made at level of ongoing transformational activity by secondary
processes." Perhaps research with poets can be brought to bear on issues of
transformation, given Gruber's (in press) claim that "the medium of poetry is
particularly well suited for the transformations between sensuous experience
and abstract thought that express the visionary function at work." More will
be said about poetry later in this chapter.

A final experimental possibility is suggested by Gruber's (1990) shadowbox research. Here the transformation is one of perspective. In a typical shadowbox, two individuals must collaborate to discover what object is responsible
for two shadows. Each individual sees only one of the shadows, and because

of their positions and limited views, the shadows are quite different from one another. A cone, for example, might create a circular shadow when the light originates from the point, and it can create a triangular shadow when the light originates from the perpendicular. Clearly the shadowbox requires a kind of discovery or insightful problem solving, and these in turn require the individuals to share their information. The transformation is apparent when they move from their own view (for example, the circular shadow or the triangle) to the integrated view. In a sense the individuals transform by accommodating the shared information.

The shadowbox might be used with parents and their children, or with children of different ages. But interestingly, transformations are also suggested when the shadowbox is used by one individual (Gruber, 1990). That person first obtains one view of some object or picture, but then obtains additional views (perhaps by moving to a different position). He or she must integrate information and construct new meaning. Note that the transformations involved are entirely personal. In fact, the individual no doubt transforms existing information rather than data from new experiences. It may be that individuals start with objective experience and derive some interpretation of it, but then subsequent transformations may involve reinterpretations, and reinterpretations of reinterpretations. I believe this parallels the process Piaget referred to as *reflective abstraction*.

Clearly, then, there are several options for empirical assessments of transformational capacities. As a general prediction for this research, transformational capacities would be expected to be fairly constant through the life span, with the possible exceptions of very early infancy and a terminal drop in late life. Developmental changes would be expected when mature creators utilize both the skill to transform external information appropriately and creatively and the discretion to know when to transform that information. Immaturity might be seen when a child indiscriminately transforms everything into an object for play or exploration. He or she might use a spoon for a drum stick, or use a shoe for a shovel, ignoring the fact that the same dirty shoe must be worn again soon. It is discretion and intentions that most clearly separate mature from immature creativity.

Discretion

Discretion is indicative of mindful choice. It must be included in definitions of creativity because it ensures that originality is distinct from useless and psychotic ideation, both of which reflect originality but at the wrong times or to an unfortunate extreme. Effectively creative individuals will transform information and thus exercise control over their experiences, but they will not transform so much that they are left with entirely useless and unrealistic information. It might be that discretion kicks in after a transformation has taken place, as Torrance (in press) suggested. He was outlining the role of emotional and "suprarational" processes in creative thinking, but he noted that once the breakthrough ideas are produced, they must be subjected to the laws of standard logic (see Noppe, in press).

Not only does an individual choose what information to use and what to ignore; he or she must make similar decisions about which *expectations* to abide by and which to ignore. Expectations are extremely powerful, especially during development. Ready examples of this can be found in a quick examination of fads and fashions: How many persons really consider the appropriateness of and their personal feelings about them? How about more important social mores and traditions? Very frequently people conform to expectations and do not mindfully consider the options (Langer, Hatem, Joss, and Howell, 1989).

I mentioned discretion earlier, distinguishing between adaptation and creativity, the former being reactive and the latter proactive. Note, however, that discretion is not purely cognitive. The choices and judgments that indicate discretion no doubt rely on cognitive process, but some of these are heuristic rather than algorithmic (Runco, Johnson, and Gaynor, in press). Additionally, the weight given to the various options within a decision tree may surprise any observer because they are so personal. The logic manifested in an individual's choices may not be at all obvious unless the values and criteria being used are known.

One obvious example of discretion is found in the choice of creative individuals to ignore conventions (Eisenman, 1992; Runco, 1993a) and behave in a *contrarian* manner. Although some conventions are vital for communication and the like, there is frequently value in contrarian actions, which break rules and traditions. Creative persons may value contrarian behavior because they know that it often leads to original insights. It is, then, a strategy for them (Rubenson, 1991) and a means toward an end that they value, that is, a creative outcome. Children can be quite unconventional (Dudek, 1974; Rosenblatt and Winner, 1988), but they are unaware of conventions rather than unconventional because of contrarian choices (Dudek, 1974).

Ludwig (1989) gave Sigmund Freud and Duke Ellington as exemplars of contrarian creators. Ludwig described how, "Knowingly or not, Ellington exploited traditional musical rules as inspiration for his jazz. If he learned that he was not supposed to use parallel fifths, he immediately would find a way to do so; if told that major sevenths must always rise, he would write a tune in which the line descended from the major seventh; and if the tritone was forbidden, he would find the earliest opportunity to use it and, to emphasize the point, would let it stand alone and exposed" (pp. 7–8).

Consider also Dr. Seuss. Many of his books rely on a unique vocabulary. Seuss often invented new words and expressions. Here is one example: "Just tell yourself, Duckie, you're really quite lucky! Some people are much more . . . oh ever so much more . . . oh, muchly much-much more unlucky than you!" (Geisel, 1973, p. 5). Geisel was in that sense breaking lexical rules, and much the same could be said about his syntax. Numerous other examples could be mentioned where creators break syntactic rules (for example, "ain't nothin' but a hound dog") or even intentionally distort reality in their work (for example, "got so much honey the bees envy me").

But creators like Geisel do not go overboard. If a creator completely disregards rules or traditions, he or she is likely to find original but unacceptable or useless ideas or solutions. In fact, I must say "likely" in that sentence because it is virtually impossible to give examples of individuals who have reputations as creative but have gone overboard. Individuals with reputations have done contrarian things, but only in the manner in which we are describing it—that is, with some discretion. Those reputable creators who use these kinds of tactics probably are careful when they break the rules and to what degree they are contrarian. It might be best to describe the first tactic as "bend the rules" instead of the more extreme "disregard the rules."

Discretion is partly heuristic cognition, and partly value judgment, the latter implied by the fact that certain criteria must be used as an individual makes choices about what to transform, what to attend to, and where to invest personal resources. You might say that individuals choose which things should be transformed, and how far things should be transformed, according to their values. For creative individuals, like Ellington and Geisel, originality is highly valued.

Significantly, the developmental patterns predicted for discretion and values suggest that development is a result of creative activity as much as it is a result. The choices often determine what is experienced, rather than vice versa. Individuals may, for example, put effort into developing their creative skills, investing time to master a body of knowledge, taking time to identify and use strategies like the contrarian and what Gruber (1988) called *deviation amplification*. These strategies are often intentionally developed and applied (McNaughton, 1995; Root-Bernstein, 1988), but the development and application of them requires effort—and that effort will not be expended unless there is a reason to do so. Creativity must be valued by the individual before investing in its enhancement.

In this light, individuals may differ in their behavior, not so much because of their abilities but because of the choices they make (Runco, Johnson, and Gaynor, in press). These choices can in turn lead to the development of abilities and strategies, as well as to specific ideas and solutions. Two persons may have the same transformational capacities, but one values interpretations that result in comfortable ideas and solutions, whereas the other uses exactly the same skills to generate creative and refreshing ideas and solutions.

This description may sound highly speculative, but the role of values and personal aesthetic criteria is consistent with the existing literature. Perkins (1984), for example, described how "creative people *strive* for originality, and for something fundamental, far-reaching, and powerful" (p. 19). Similarly, Welsh (1975) defined creativity in terms of the ability to bring new things into being, and "modify one's environment in accordance with aesthetic criteria" (quoted in Gough and Heilbrun, 1980, p. 24). Abra's view of innovation (in press), quoted earlier, is again pertinent. Most likely an individual innovates at least in part because of an interest in improving something.

The idea of discretion is also consistent with the view presented by Collingwood (1972) and recently interpreted by Anderson and Hausman (1992, p. 299) in which "aesthetic emotion indicates a way in which it . . . can function as a guide during and at the completion of an artist's activity of expressing him or herself imaginatively." Anderson and Hausman specifically tied aesthetic emotions to the individual's control, and both "control" and the idea of an aesthetic as a guide support the role of discretion.

Barron (1993) intimated something about discretion in his comments on poetry. He suggested that poetry is "perhaps the most exacting discipline in the search through memory for combinations that will express new ideas. . . . A poem can be marvelously intricate, and, in fact, the more intricate, very often the more simple the effect. . . . The most powerful of poetic images are multi-dimensional. They are deep as well as broad, they have intensity, they are evocative of a wider range of responsive images in the reader or hearer. *And, they are not 'overly so,' they are 'just so.' . . . They are not overinclusive; that would make poor poetry*" (pp. 182–183, emphasis added).

Barron was particularly critical of the theory that creative thinking is related to overinclusive thinking (see Eysenck, 1993, in press) and indicated that creativity requires an optimum, or what he called *controlled weirdness*. This is a good term for the discretionary transformation in the interpretive definition of this chapter.

Gruber (1978) recognized the role of a personal aesthetic when he described the connection individuals feel with their work. In his words, "attachment comes with its attendant access to the person's whole value system . . .[and] may help to explain an otherwise quite puzzling experience. When we hear of a new idea or a new finding, we often know with a sense of great immediacy that it 'feels right' or that it 'feels wrong.' Only later do we work out our reasons" (p. 138). This ties the personal aesthetic to values and intuition.

The connections among originality, unconventionality, autonomy, contrarian strategies, and creativity might suggest that these are universal criteria used by all creative individuals. This is not a necessary assumption, nor am I entirely comfortable with it myself; however, there is some indication that creative persons very frequently appreciate originality and its correlates, and question conventions. The universality of metaphor, noted earlier, is relevant here (Gibbs, in press). If that is not enough, consider the range of other universal developmental tendencies that have been predicted. Kohlberg (1987), for example, described a *universal ethic* as a part of moral development. Even more directly relevant is Frois and Eysenck's (1995) theory of a *universal aesthetic* (p. 4), which they supported with data from the Visual Aesthetic Test, judgments from which were independent of culture and even artistic training. Universality is implied by the lack of differences among cultures.

Hofstadter (1985) implied that creativity has a universal base when he proposed that "'To dream things that never were'—this is not just poetic phrase [from George Bernard Shaw], but a truth about human nature. Even the dullest of us is endowed with this strange ability to come up with counterfactual worlds and to dream" (p. 232). Pearlman (1983) pointed to a fit or whole implied by a set of satisfied criteria that makes a creative product aesthetically pleasing (p. 295). Most telling may be Feldman, Csikszentmihalyi, and Gardner's (1994) implied universality in their view of the *transformational imperative*. This brings us to the last part of the interpretive definition of creativity, namely intentionality.

Intentions

The role of intentions in creative work is a matter of much debate. This debate is exacerbated by the fact that intentions are related to the larger issue of chance; if creative work is dependent on chance factors, then it is not guaranteed regardless of the clarity and potency of one's intentions (see Albert, 1988; Gruber, 1988; Simonton, 1988).

Hofstadter (1985) argued against the significance of intentions when he wrote, "Invention is much more like falling off a log than like sawing one in two. Despite Thomas Alva Edison's memorable remark, 'Genius is 2 percent inspiration and 98 percent perspiration,' we're not all going to become geniuses simply by sweating more or resolving to *try harder*. A mind follows the path of least resistance, and it's when it feels easiest that it is most likely to be creative. . . . Trying harder is not the name of the game; the trick is getting the right concept to begin with, so that making variations on it is like taking candy from a baby" (p. 233). Hofstadter seemed to appreciate problem identification with that comment about starting with the right concept, and he went on to define creativity as the making of variations on a theme, which would seem to be another way of describing transformations. In those points his view fits the definition presented in this chapter, but what is striking in the quotation is that he downplays personal intentions and efforts. So much for motivation!

Khatena and Khatena (1990), in contrast, were supportive of intentions, and in fact they suggested a connection specifically between intentions and metaphor use. They pointed out that individuals often try to "simulate the [creative] impulse" (p. 21) rather than waiting passively for inspiration. They also tied metaphors specifically to transformations, which supports the definition offered in this chapter. It also fits with the claim of Gibbs (in press) that "poets often write for the express purpose of creating disturbing new images, ones that result from mappings of image structures from widely disparate domains" (p. 209). This express purpose reinforces my argument about intentionality, and the "disturbing images" would seem to support the idea that creators value the unconventional and contrarian.

Intentionality suggests that the work starts with the person. Different directions of effect were recognized by Parnes (1987), who contrasted "let it happen" and "make it happen" strategies for creative work. Similarly, Richards (1994) was specific about direction of effect when she described "the pull of the aesthetic," and she even tied it to transformation: "Aesthetic appeal, broadly defined, may even serve as a deliberate *draw*—inviting us to come closer, perhaps to act. It urges us to notice and remember, to think, to process and transform, and thereby somehow to be creative ourselves" (Richards, 1995).

For obvious reasons I am marshaling theories and hypotheses that are consistent with the tripartite interpretive definition of creativity, but I at this point I should mention the debate about the possibility that young children are only accidentally—and thus unintentionally—creative. As Wolf and Larson (1981) described it, for example, young children may not know what is appropriate, and as a result they tend to say and do surprising things. To give an example close to home, my four-year-old son drew a wonderful picture of a house—with four chimneys, because if one chimney is good (he believes in Santa), four must be better. Only two of the chimneys were vertical; two were connected to the siding of his house. Adults see things like this as original, and often infer that the child in question is creative, but in fact Wolf and Larson suggest that the child simply does not know better. A similar view was given by Dudek (1974), though she emphasized children's lack of expressiveness.

Children can be intentionally strategic in their creative efforts. This is implied by findings from research on *explicit instructions,* which are simply very clear directions for how to find original or creative ideas (Harrington, 1975). Of particular interest is Runco's (1986) finding that gifted children do not benefit as much as nongifted children when given explicit instructions to be original ("give ideas that no one else will"). One explanation for this is that the gifted children were spontaneously looking for original ideas and thus did not benefit from the instructions. Davidson and Sternberg (1983) also reported finding spontaneous strategies for gifted children, and the experimenters relied on insight problems, which can easily be indicative of cognitive restructuring.

Several others have discussed the role of intentions in creative work. Rothenberg (1990a), for example, described the significance of "aesthetic purpose" and "aesthetic intent." He also described how the intentional use of two processes—the *janusian* and *homospatial*—may have contributed to the insights of Niels Bohr, Soren Kierkegaard, Albert Einstein, and many others (Rothenberg, 1990b). Janusian thinking involves the integration of antitheses; homospatial thinking involves integrations of images that do not naturally occupy the same space. In addition to biographical support, Rothenberg presented findings from several laboratory studies (reviewed in Rothenberg, 1990b, in press). Importantly, Rothenberg insisted that the deliberate and intentional character of these processes distinguishes them from less healthy forms of thought (for example, regression). It also ties them to the definition I presented earlier. Rothenberg's (1990a) experimental techniques for the study of homospatial thinking might be added to the list of available methodologies I mentioned earlier in this chapter, but then again he recommended their use only for adolescence and thereafter.

Feldman, Csikszentmihalyi, and Gardner (1994) recognized intentions in their recent theory of creativity, and they too emphasized transformations. They saw intentionality when individuals "believe in the possibility of making changes to better achieve our [human] ends" (p. 31), which sounds like transformational innovations. They further proposed that individuals "imagine changes that might actually be brought into existence and placed into the crafted world of human culture . . . [for this] is what must occur for creativity to be possible. This kind of thinking could only occur if it is pushed by a 'transformational imperative' born of unconscious experience of the power to bring about changes beyond current reality constraints" (pp. 32–33).

Another view that is remarkably compatible with the interpretive definition was presented by Schwebel (1993). He defined moral creativity in the arts as "the conscious transformation of moral values and their associated affect into artistic products" (p. 68). This emphasis on art is more specific than that implied by my definition; but then again Schwebel's view of art as a means for "satisfying human needs" implies a universality, and morals assume values. Schwebel also shares my interest in development. He described eight phases of the development of moral creativity, which begins with a lack of awareness about interpersonal relations, moves to awareness of both inter- and intrapersonal issues and subsequent reflections about them, and indicates maturity with "full integration at the conscious and unconscious levels of experience of using one's creative powers for pure art, perhaps achieving aesthetic refinements of dehumanized abstractions" (p. 70).

Barron (1995) was well aware of the need for intentional transformations when he described *transcendence* and the creative "ability to create ourselves and to evolve by our own design through reflection upon the changes we bring about." Intentionality is implied by the fact that changes may be of our own design. Barron extended this line of thought when he described free will: "The essence of our human freedom is this, that matter has acquired the capacity to work radical modifications in itself. Thus, among its 'available responses' is the ability to act in such a manner as to increase its own flexibility, or deliberately to maximize its own response variability" (p. 84).

Numerous other examples of creativity relying on deliberate and intentional decisions were reported by Runco, Johnson, and Gaynor (in press). They cited examples from various areas, including the preference for complexity, career choices, and the styles used by artists. The first of these could be added to our list of values and criteria—creative persons seem to appreciate complexity (Barron, 1995; Eisenman, 1992)—but the last may be the most pertinent because particular developmental trends have been identified, including the *late life style* (see Arnheim, 1990; Cohen-Shalev, 1989; Lindauer, 1992, 1993).

Discussion and Implications

At this point it should be clear that there is plenty of theorizing and some data about each of the three components of creativity, as it was defined in the early part of this chapter. It should also be clear that this definition, emphasizing transformations, discretion, and intentions, can be applied to the creativity of children as well as adults. Most important may be the transformational skill. This gives children the cognitive mechanism for creative thinking and insight, even if they lack the discretion or intentions of adolescents and adults. In the remainder of the chapter I discuss the role of experience and knowledge. I also discuss the implications of the interpretive definition of creativity, and I attempt to further distinguish the interpretive basis from related processes (for example, perception).

Knowledge and Experience

Surely many persons lack the knowledge that is necessary for expertise and high-level achievement. Still, to the degree that knowledge is a function of learning, individuals who have the intentions emphasized in my definition will invest the time necessary for the acquisition of sufficient knowledge bases. This applies to both factual, declarative knowledge and to procedural, strategic knowledge, and thus to metacognition (Runco and Chand, 1994). Admittedly, it is not always useful to distinguish between cognition and metacognition, for both are based on information. Nor is it always best to distinguish between cognition and affect; often the latter has a basis in the former. Runco (1993b, 1994a, 1994b) suggested this with intrinsic motivation—a correlate of intentions—as his example.

Albert (1990, p. 19) described the role of knowledge this way:

> Creativity begins with and is expressed through the decisions one makes, not through the particular media used or the products generated. . . . An individual's knowledge of self and particular aspects of his or her world is the ultimate medium of creative behavior, for knowledge determines decisions as much as opportunities. In fact, it is on the basis of one's knowledge that one can perceive and identify one's opportunities. To the extent that deliberate efforts and decisions have to be made in career choices and performances, then to that degree one can say that personalized knowledge is a major component of creative and eminence-achieving work.

Note Albert's attention to deliberate (that is, intentional) efforts.

Direct experience can supply useful knowledge, but clearly a balance must be struck: The individual needs to benefit from experience, but at the same time avoid relying on it. Indeed, recent research suggests that forgetting can be good (Riccio, Rabinowitz, and Axelrod, 1994). If individuals constantly attend to the numerous details provided by each new experience, they would have no time for concentration or relaxation and incubation. If, on the other hand, they rely entirely on past experience, their actions will be automatized and rigid. They lose their ability to make choices, to use their discretion. As Barron (1995) described it, "the more fully developed and finely articulated we become, the less the *opportunity for alternative integration*" (emphasis in original). He referred to this as "one of the basic paradoxes of human development." Maturity often brings rigidity and automatization, and flexibility can be lost, probably in proportion to truly mindful choice (Langer, 1989; Rubenson and Runco, 1995). Advanced development void of creativity is manifested as an increased dependence on conventions and routine. No room for discretion there.

Just as a balance must be found between experience and naïveté, so too must there be a balance between maturity and immaturity, the rational and nonrational, play and serious work, the divergent and evaluative, the personal and social, and the subjective and objective. That balance may shift and discretion may give the creator a sense of timing so he or she knows when to be original and when to be more conventional—but it is a balance, an optimization. Runco and Sakamoto (1996) went into more detail about the concept of optimization as it applies to creativity.

In some ways, the balance among rational and what Torrance (in press) called the *suprarational* cannot be controlled by the creative individual or, in the case of youth, by their parents, teachers, and mentors. Yet creative persons do exert great influence on their development; their behavior and manifest talent often elicit certain experiences. Scarr and McCartney referred to this as *evocative development* (also see Albert and Runco, 1989). It does complicate the aforementioned direction of effect issue. Consider, for example, the creative individuals whose talents dramatically influence their experience (for example, parents move to allow talented youth to study with an appropriate mentor or coach) but whose talents are in fact at least partly dependent on their experiences. Add to this the possibility that the individual feels the "pull of the aesthetic" (Richards, 1994), in which case the locus of control shifts outward, away from the creator. That same outward shift would be very apparent in creative individuals who "let it happen" rather than "make it happen" (Parnes, 1987), or who simply await inspiration. All of this may seem abstract, but then again it is very relevant to our understanding of the motivation for and development of creativity.

There are also biological givens (Albert, in press), which at the very least set the *range of reaction* within which talents must develop. Additionally, there are certain experiences that are simply beyond control. These are epitomized in traumatic experiences, which do seem to characterize the childhoods of many creative individuals (Albert and Elliot, 1973; Runco, 1994a).

Psychoanalytic theories often tie such traumas to the development of creative talent. Not surprisingly, when they do, they usually point to a kind of transformation that is in some ways similar to the mental operation I have described. Rank (1932), for example, stated that artists must struggle with and resolve the profound conflict between self and society in order to reach their creative potential, and some psychodynamic theorists have argued that creative achievement is a compensation for deep personal problems (Freud, 1924) or inferiorities (Adler, see Sheldon, 1995). The classic Freudian view emphasizes *sublimation,* a defense mechanism that transforms inner conflict into socially acceptable works and symbols, including art. Significantly, the transformations hypothesized by psychoanalytic theory may be unintentional. They are in this sense different from those I have described in this chapter.

They are also related to questionable psychological health. That assertion is in clear contrast to the humanistic view of creativity as an indication of exceptional psychological.health (Maslow, 1971; Rogers, 1959). It is also largely inconsistent with the very interesting findings about "illusions of mental health" (Richards, 1994). Miller and Porter (1988), for example, predicted that depressive individuals "would attribute negative events to internal, stable, global causes and positive events to external, unstable, and specific causes. . . . [But] it was the depressives in these studies who displayed rationality and accuracy! *Depressed people were more realistic.* It was the nondepressives who exhibited an *illusion of control,* or what can be called an *optimistic bias*" (quoted in Heinzen, 1994, p. 73). Certain illusions may reflect the creative interpretations made possible by the transformations I described above.

Mraz and Runco (1994) argued that creativity would minimize the probability of suicide and stress. As they described it, when individuals take external information and transform it into a personally interpretable structure, they may perceive objective life events, or "stressors," but not experience stress. In the terms of Mraz and Runco, creative transformations moderate objective and subjective experiences, and creative individuals are more likely to see alternatives and solve problems in a flexible fashion. With that in mind, they suggested that creative individuals would be less likely to consider suicide a serious option. An uncreative person might, on the other hand, see few alternatives and thus see suicide as worthy of consideration. Mraz and Runco presented empirical findings that suicide ideation is associated with fluent problem identification and rigid problem solving. This hypothesized bridge between creativity and suicide ideation is quite significant given the increases in the number of children and adolescents who are attempting suicide or experiencing great stress (Carson and others, 1992; Elkind, 1983). Perhaps specific counseling techniques could benefit from creativity training procedures.

Two other implications of the interpretive definition of creativity should be mentioned. One entails moral reasoning. The connection here is the common emphasis on intentions. Gruber (1993a), for example, proposed that "ought implies can implies create," the key message being that "whenever we assert that something 'ought' to be the case, we presuppose that it is possible, that it can be done. Furthermore, once we know that something ought and can be done, action is called for" (p. 5). Runco (1993a) explored the role of intentions in creative work by examining the concept of *subjective moral reasoning* and its parallel in the creative domain. Simplifying somewhat, subjective moral reasoning assumes that morality can be judged by taking intentions into account. Creative persons are often quite rebellious, but with moral or ethical intentions.

The interpretive definition of creativity also has implications for education. Educators can, for instance, target specific facets of creative potential, such as transformational thinking, discretion and choice, and personal interpretations. Piaget (1976) can be cited once again in this regard. He suggested that "to understand is to discover, or reconstruct by rediscovery, and such conditions must be complied with if in the future individuals are to be formed who are capable of production and creativity and not simply recognition" (p. 20). Piaget would have education focus on personal inventions and constructions. Much the same is implied by the interpretive theory proposed herein.

Keep in mind that the interpretive theory of creativity is strikingly different from Piagetian theory in two ways. The first was mentioned earlier: Piagetian theory typically assumes thinking and problem solving to employ conventional or even formal logic (see Feldman, 1994; Levine, 1984). Creative thinking and problem solving, in contrast, may require a break from convention and what I called metaphoric logic. The second difference may be merely one of emphasis. I refer to the definition with transformation, discretion, and intentions as the *interpretive definition,* but in Piagetian terms it is a kind of assimilation. Many other theories of creativity, and particularly those that equate creativity with insight, place emphasis on new structures and thus on accommodation, not assimilation.

If the tendency to transform experience indeed represents a cognitive preference, or even a kind of cognitive style, it may be stable enough and used frequently enough to contribute to major insights and cognitive restructuring. That contribution would be consistent with Piaget's (1976) position that assimilation and accommodation *work together* for adaptation. The transformation in the interpretive definition no doubt could also complement the cognitive restructuring aspects of creative thinking described by Mumford and Gustafson (in press), Ohlsson (1984), and Gruber (1988). Still, just as Piaget (1976) distinguished between assimilation and accommodation, so too should the distinction between moment-to-moment interpretations and major cognitive restructuring be retained, at least for theory development and educational applications. Those interested in early development may need to focus on the former. These will be especially helpful for studies of children and for studies of everyday creativity (for example, Runco and Richards, in press).

Even though I have focused on interpretations rather than more significant changes in cognitive restructuring, my definition fits into the constructivist category, assumptions for which are questioned by Sampson (1988) and Goswami (in press), the latter focusing on creativity. Theoretical and empirical support for a constructivist approach was given by Gruber (1981), Mumford and Gustafson (in press), and Ohlsson (1984).

Arguably, a developmental definition should focus on the everyday interpretation of experience rather than on major intellectual breakthroughs. Major breakthroughs, like those responsible for paradigm shifts (Kuhn, 1963), are of course quite important. But original interpretations of experience are, too, in part because they are so common, even in the lives of very young children. It should be clear at this juncture that they also have important implications for morality (Gruber, 1993a; Runco, 1993a), innovation (Abra, in press; Barron,

1995; Feldman, Csikszentmihalyi, and Gardner, 1994), health (Mraz and Runco, 1994; Richards, 1994), and education (Levine, 1984; Piaget, 1976b).

The logic used in many creative efforts was called metaphorical in part because of the widely-recognized connection between analogical or metaphorical thinking and creativity. *Metaphorical* is certainly a better label than arational or nonrational, at least in the sense the these processes are not lacking in logic. They simply have a logic of their own—often a personal logic, and one that may not seem logical in an objective sense. Here again we are close to psychoanalytical theory, which might be interpreted as suggesting that the unconscious has a logic of its own.

I bring metaphor up once again because it is related to one of the least tractable problems in the area of creativity research, namely the judgment of creative persons or products. If creative insights are personally or metaphorically logical and fitting, identification and judgment by others are very difficult. This is precisely why some creativity scholars suggest that we devote our efforts to unambiguous cases of creativity. If they are unambiguous, by definition their logic is objectively obvious. Elsewhere I have argued against this view (Runco, 1995, in press), as did Maslow (1971) who was quoted several times earlier in this chapter. Given our developmental concerns here, I should reiterate that the study only of unambiguous cases of creativity would preclude studies of children, of potential at any age level, and of everyday instances of creativity. I am also concerned that studies of unambiguous cases would take us away from the heart of the matter, the mechanism by which creative individuals find their appropriately creative ideas.

Granted, creativity will not be well understood just as a cognitive mechanism; it is also emotional or affective. I think the affect is assumed by the notion of personal logic, but much more can be said about emotions and the other extracognitive bases of creative thinking. Autonomy, for example, contributes to the capacity of the creative persons to think in an original and unconventional fashion; it allows them at least to postpone conformity to expectations and the like (Shalley, 1991). Not surprisingly, autonomy is one of the most commonly noted characteristics of creative persons (Albert and Runco, 1989). It is closely tied to the unconventionality mentioned several times in this chapter, to the *mindfulness* Langer, Hatem, Joss, and Howell (1989) related to creativity and education, and at the extreme, to the deviance that is increasingly recognized in theories of creativity (Eisenman, 1992; Richards, 1994). Richards' work on this topic is very important, for she shows how deviation ensures variation, and how variation in turn supports adaptiveness on personal and societal levels.

There is a longer view of adaptation. It focuses on the adaptation of groups, or even the human species, and thus it can maintain the bridge between adaptiveness and creativity. In this view creative behavior is unconventional, and that means that it ensures variation among individuals (Richards, 1994). Such variation is conducive to evolution and progress. Note the educational implications of this view. One of the most obvious is simply that teachers should be appreciative of individual differences, even if some students are quite unconventional.

Barron (1995) claimed that "creative individuals retain qualities of freshness, spontaneity, and joy, as well as a certain lack of reality-testing—openness to the non-rational, if you will. They are in that sense childlike, but this is not regression; it is progression with courage. They bring their childhood along instead of leaving it behind." This is noteworthy in part because it is compatible with the idea that creative thinking allows creativity to reflect both childlike and quite mature abilities and tendencies. It is also noteworthy because it underscores the nonrational as well as the concept of affect—the latter in Barron's idea about courage.

Such courage may follow directly from ego strength. A strong ego will allow variations and weirdness, but will support the discretion to keep the individual from going overboard (see Kris, 1952; Noppe, in press). Ego strength is often necessary because creative ideas and insights can be frightening, so an individual will not only need to decide to explore or take advantage of them but must be capable of tolerating them. Rothenberg (1990b) discussed the fear that might be associated with or result specifically from creative insights. Along the same lines Schuldberg (1994) discussed the "personal access to simultaneous, contradictory emotions [that] can provide an important and even necessary component of creative work."

Final Comments

The definition I offered early in this chapter is supported by the distinctions already described, including those between creativity and innovation, between creativity and adaptation, between creativity and problem solving, and between what I have called the moment-to-moment quality of creative interpretations, on one hand, and the more stable cognitive restructuring process, on the other.

One final distinction should be presented. This is the one between perceptual and the more discretionary processes. Smith and Amner (in press) described their *percept-genesis* research, which is very useful for explorations of the interplay of the preconscious and conscious involved in the construction of meaningful interpretations. Smith and Carlsson (1983) concluded that young children will lack the ability to distinguish between fantasy and reality, and they argued that true creativity first appears during preadolescence. Rothenberg (1990a) concurred, and not coincidentally his research on homospatial process has a perceptual slant. Granted, the perceptual basis of creativity is very relevant to the interpretive and transformational basis I am defending. Perception can be distinguished from simple sensation precisely because it involves an interpretation, the latter involving only the detection of stimuli. Perception and creative insight are, then, both interpretive—but the latter requires originality in addition to meaningfulness. Perhaps we can view perception as requiring interpretations that are sometimes original, and creativity as requiring original insights that are sometimes widely meaningful. If nothing else, we can fall back on intentionality; perceptual processes are much less governed by one's intentions than are other creative processes.

Once the role of transformations and interpretation in creative thinking is more widely recognized, and if we move from the present emphasis on socially recognized products to process and mechanism, appropriate developmental studies will no doubt be conducted. As suggested earlier, this research might take advantage of the existing literature on transformation as a cognitive acquisition (Kavanaugh and Harris, 1994) and the methods used to study pretending (Harris, 1994), percept genesis (Smith and Amner, in press), janusian and homospatial processes (Rothenberg, 1990b), and the shadowbox (Gruber, 1990). The definition proposed in this chapter, with its emphasis on transformations, discretion, and intentions, gives us several choices for further research on creativity as advanced development and an opportunity to get close to the mechanism that underlies creative thinking across the life span.

References

Abra, J. "Changes in Creativity with Age: Data, Explanations, and Further Predictions." *International Journal of Aging and Human Development,* 1989, *28,* 105–126.

Abra, J. *The Motives for Creative Work: An Inquiry.* Cresskill, N.J.: Hampton Press, in press.

Albert, R. S. "How High Must We Climb to Reach Higher Ground?" *Creativity Research Journal,* 1988, *1.*

Albert, R. S. "Identity, Experiences, and Career Choice Among the Exceptionally Gifted and Eminent." In M. A. Runco and R. S. Albert (eds.), *Theories of Creativity.* Thousand Oaks, Calif.: Sage, 1990.

Albert, R. S. "The Achievement of Eminence as an Evolutionary Strategy." In M. A. Runco (ed.), *Creativity Research Handbook,* Vol. 2. Cresskill, N.J.: Hampton Press, in press.

Albert, R. S., and Elliot, R. C. "Creative Ability and the Handling of Personal and Social Conflict Among Bright Sixth Graders." *Journal of Social Behavior and Personality,* 1973, *1,* 169–181.

Albert, R. S., and Runco, M. A. "Independence and Cognitive Ability in Gifted and Exceptionally Gifted Boys." *Journal of Youth and Adolescence,* 1989, *18,* 221–230.

Anderson, D. R., and Hausman, C. R. "The Role of Aesthetic Emotion in R. G. Collingwood's Conception of Creative Activity." *Journal of Aesthetics and Art Criticism,* 1992, *50,* 299–305.

Arnheim, R. "On the Late Style." In M. Perlmutter (ed.), *Late Life Potential.* Washington, D.C.: Gerontological Society of America, 1990.

Bachelor, P., and Michael, W. B. "Higher-Order Factors of Creativity Within Guilford's Structure-of-Intellect Model: A Re-Analysis of a 53 Variable Data Base." *Creativity Research Journal,* 1991.

Barron, F. "Controllable Oddness as a Resource in Creativity." *Psychological Inquiry,* 1993, *4,* 182–184.

Barron, F. *No Rootless Flower: An Ecology of Creativity.* Cresskill, N.J.: Hampton Press, 1995.

Berlyne, D. E. *Conflict, Arousal, and Curiosity.* New York: McGraw-Hill, 1960.

Boniger, D. S., Gleicher, F., and Strathman, A. "Counterfactual Thinking: From What Might Have Been to What May Be." *Journal of Personality and Social Psychology,* in press.

Carson, D. K., and others. "Creative Thinking as a Predictor of School-Aged Children's Stress Responses and Coping Abilities." *Creativity Research Journal,* 1992, *7,* 145–158.

Charlton, J. *A Little Learning Is a Dangerous Thing.* New York: St. Martin's Press, 1994.

Clement, J. "Observed Method for Generating Analogies in Scientific Problem Solving." *Cognitive Science,* 1988, *12,* 563–586.

Cohen, L. "Continuum of Adaptive Creative Behaviors." *Creativity Research Journal,* 1989, 2, 169–183.

Cohen-Shalev, A. "Old Age Style: Developmental Changes in Creative Production from a Life-Span Perspective." *Journal of Aging Studies,* 1989, 3, 21–37.

Collingwood, R. G. *The Principles of Art.* New York: Oxford University Press, 1972.

Davidson, J. E., and Sternberg, R. J. "The Role of Insight in Intellectual Giftedness." *Gifted Child Quarterly,* 1983, 28, 58–64.

Davis, S. N., Keegan, R. T., and Gruber, H. E. "Creativity as Purposeful Work: The Evolving Systems Approach." In M. A. Runco (ed.), *Creativity Research Handbook,* Vol. 1. Cresskill, N.J.: Hampton Press, in press.

Dudek, S. Z. "Creativity in Young Children: Attitude or Ability?" *Journal of Creative Behavior,* 1974, 8, 282–292.

Dudek, S. Z. "Aesthetics and Art." In M. A. Runco (ed.), *Creativity Research Handbook,* Vol. 2. Cresskill, N.J.: Hampton Press, in press.

Dudek, S. Z., and Verreault, R. "The Creative Thinking and Ego Functioning of Children." *Creativity Research Journal,* 1989, 2, 64–86.

Eisenman, R. "Creativity in Prisoners: Conduct Disorders and Psychotics." *Creativity Research Journal,* 1992, 5, 175–182.

Elkind, D. *Child and Society.* New York: Oxford University Press, 1979.

Elkind, D. *The Hurried Child.* Reading, Mass.: Addison-Wesley, 1983.

Epstein, S., Lipson, A., Holstein, C., and Huh, E. "Irrational Reactions to Negative Outcomes: Evidence for Two Conceptual Systems." *Journal of Personality and Social Psychology,* 1992, 62, 328–339.

Eysenck, H. J. "Creativity and Personality: Suggestions for a Theory." *Psychological Inquiry,* 1993, 4, 147–178.

Eysenck, H. J. In M. A. Runco (ed.), *Critical Creative Processes.* Cresskill, N.J.: Hampton Press, in press.

Feldman, D. H. "Creativity: Dreams, Insights, and Transformations." In D. H. Feldman, M. Csikszentmihalyi, and H. Gardner (eds.), *Changing the World: A Framework for the Study of Creativity.* Westport, Conn.: Praeger, 1994.

Feldman, D. H., Csikszentmihalyi, M., and Gardner, H. "A Framework for the Study of Creativity." In D. H. Feldman, M. Csikszentmihalyi, and H. Gardner (eds.), *Changing the World: A Framework for the Study of Creativity.* Westport, Conn.: Praeger, 1994.

Feldman, D., Marrinan, B. M., and Hartfeldt, S. D. "Transformational Power as a Possible Index of Creativity." *Psychological Reports,* 1972, 30, 335–338.

Flach, F. "Disorders of the Pathways Involved in the Creative Process." *Creativity Research Journal,* 1990, 3, 158–165.

Freud, S. "The Relation of the Poet to Day-Dreaming." In *Collected Papers,* Vol. 4. London: Hogarth Press, 1924.

Frois, J. P., and Eysenck, H. J. "The Visual Aesthetic Sensitivity Test as Applied to Portuguese Children and Fine Arts Students." *Creativity Research Journal,* 1995, 8.

Gardner, H. *Art, Mind, and Brain.* New York: Basic Books, 1982.

Gardner, H. *Creating Minds: An Anatomy of Creativity Seen Through the Lives of Freud, Einstein, Picasso, Stravinsky, Eliot, Graham, and Gandhi.* New York: Basic Books, 1994.

Geisel, T. S. *Did I Ever Tell You How Lucky You Are?* by Dr. Seuss. New York: Random House, 1973.

Gibbs, R. W., Jr. "Metaphoric Transformations in Understanding Artistic Creations." In A. Montuori (ed.), *Unusual Associates: Essays in Honor of Frank Barron.* Cresskill, N.J.: Hampton Press, in press.

Goswami, A. "Creativity and the Quantum: Toward a Unified Theory." *Creativity Research Journal,* in press.

Gough, H. G., and Heilbrun, A. B. *The Adjective Check List Manual.* Palo Alto, Calif.: Consulting Psychologists Press, 1980.

Gruber, H. E. "Darwin's 'Tree of Nature' and Other Images of Wide Scope." In J. Wechsler (ed.), *On Aesthetics in Science.* Cambridge, Mass.: MIT Press, 1978.

Gruber, H. E. "On the Relation Between 'Aha Experiences' and the Construction of Ideas." *History of Science,* 1981, *19,* 41–59.

Gruber, H. E. "The Evolving Systems Approach to Creative Work." *Creativity Research Journal,* 1988, *1,* 27–51.

Gruber, H. E. "The Cooperative Synthesis of Disparate Points of View." In I. Rock (ed.), *The Legacy of Solomon Asch: Essays in Cognition and Social Psychology.* Hillsdale, N.J.: Erlbaum, 1990.

Gruber, H. E. "Creativity in the Moral Domain: Ought Implies Can Implies Create." *Creativity Research Journal,* 1993a, *6,* 3–15.

Gruber, H. E. *Jean Piaget's Ideas About Creativity.* Paper presented at the meeting of the American Psychological Association, Toronto, Aug. 1993b.

Gruber, H. E., "The Life Space of a Scientist: The Visionary Function and Other Aspects of Jean Piaget's Thinking." *Creativity Research Journal,* in press.

Guilford, J. P. "Transformation Abilities or Functions." *Journal of Creative Behavior,* 1983, *17,* 75–83.

Harrington, D. M. "Effects of Explicit Instructions to be Creative on the Psychological Meaning of Divergent Test Scores." *Journal of Personality,* 1975, *43,* 434–454.

Harris, P. L. "The Child's Understanding of Emotion: Developmental Change and the Family Environment." *Journal of Child Psychology and Psychiatry,* 1994, *33,* 3–28.

Heinzen, T. "Situational Affect: Proactive and Reactive Creativity." In M. P. Shaw and M. A. Runco (eds.), *Creativity and Affect.* Norwood, N.J.: Ablex, 1994.

Hofstadter, D. *Metamagical Themas: Questing for the Essence of Mind and Patterns.* New York: Bantam Books, 1985.

Jackson, P. W. and Messick, S. "The Person, the Product, and the Response: Conceptual Problems in the Assessment of Creativity." In J. Kagan (ed.), *Creativity and Learning.* Boston: Beacon Press, 1967.

Jones, K. Unpublished doctoral dissertation. United States International University, San Diego,1995.

Kasof, J. "Explaining Creativity." *Creativity Research Journal,* 1995, *8,* 311–366.

Kavanaugh, R. D., and Harris, P. L. "Imagining the Outcome of Pretend Transformations: Assessing the Competence of Normal Children and Children with Autism." *Developmental Psychology,* 1994, *30,* 847–854.

Khatena, J., and Khatena, N. "Metaphor Motifs and Creative Imagination in Art." *Metaphor and Symbolic Activity,* 1990, *5,* 21–34.

Khattab, A. M., Michael, W. B., and Hocevar, D. "The Construct Validity of Higher Order Structure of Intellect Abilities in a Battery of Tests Emphasizing the Product of Transformations: A Confirmatory Maximum Likelihood Factor Analysis." *Educational and Psychological Measurement,* 1982, *42,* 1090–1105.

Kohlberg, L. "The Development of Moral Judgment and Moral Action." In L. Kohlberg (ed.), *Child Psychology and Childhood Education: A Cognitive Developmental View.* New York: Longman, 1987.

Kris, E. *Psychoanalytic Explorations in Art.* Madison, Conn.: International Universities Press, 1952.

Kuhn, T. "The Essential Tension: Tradition and Innovation in Scientific Research." In C. W. Taylor and F. Barron (eds.), *Scientific Creativity: Its Recognition and Development.* New York: Wiley, 1963.

Langer, E. *Mindfulness.* Reading, Mass.: Addison-Wesley, 1989.

Langer, E., Hatem, M., Joss, J., and Howell, M. "Conditional Teaching and Mindful Learning: The Role of Uncertainty in Education." *Creativity Research Journal,* 1989, *2,* 139–150.

Levine, S. H. "A Critique of the Piagetian Presuppositions of the Role of Play in Human Development and a Suggested Alternative: Metaphoric Logic Which Organizes the Play

Experience Is the Foundation for Rational Creativity." *Journal of Creative Behavior*, 1984, *18*, 90–108.

Lindauer, M. S. "Creativity in Aging Artists: Contributions from the Humanities to the Psychology of Old Age." *Creativity Research Journal*, 1992, *5*, 211–231.

Lindauer, M. S. "The Span of Creativity Among Long-Lived Historical Artists." *Creativity Research Journal*, 1993, *6*, 221–239.

Ludwig, A. "Reflections on Creativity and Madness." *American Journal of Psychotherapy*, 1989, *18*, 4–14.

MacKinnon, D. W. "The Highly Effective Individual." *Teachers College Record*, 1960, *61*, 376–378.

March, J. G. "The Technology of Foolishness." In J. G. March and J. P. Olsen (eds.), *Ambiguity and Choice in Organizations*. Bergen, Norway: Universitets-Forlaget, 1987.

Martindale, C. *The Clockwork Muse*. New York: Basic, 1990.

Martinsen, O. "Cognitive Styles and Experience in Solving Insight Problems: A Replication and Extension." *Creativity Research Journal*, 1995, *8*, 291–298.

Maslow, A. H. *The Farther Reaches of Human Nature*. New York: Viking Penguin, 1971.

McNaughton, K. (ed.). "Creativity and Discovery in the Biomedical Sciences." *Creativity Research Journal*, 1995 (special issue), *7*, 3, 4.

Mednick, S. A. "The Associative Basis of the Creative Process." *Psychological Bulletin*, 1962, *69*, 220–232.

Miller, D., and Porter, C. "Errors and Biases in the Attributional Process." In L. Y. Abramson, (ed.), *Social Cognition and Clinical Psychology*. New York: Guilford, 1988.

Mraz, W., and Runco, M. A. "Suicide Ideation and Creative Problem Solving." *Suicide and Life Threatening Behavior*, 1994, *24*, 38–47.

Mumford, M. D., and Gustafson, S. "Creativity Syndrome." *Psychological Bulletin*, 1988, *103*, 27–43.

Mumford, M. D., and Gustafson, S. "Creative Thought: Cognition and Problem Solving in Dynamic Systems." In M. A. Runco (ed.), *Creativity Research Handbook*, Vol. 2. Cresskill, N.J.: Hampton Press, in press.

Noppe, L. "Progression in the Service of the Ego." *Creativity Research Journal*, in press.

Ohlsson, S. "Restructuring Revisited." *Scandinavian Journal of Psychology*, 1984, *25*, 65–78.

O'Quin, K., and Besemer, S. P. "The Development, Reliability, and Validity of the Revised Creativity Product Semantic Scale. *Creativity Research Journal*, 1989, *2*, 267–278.

Parnes, S. *Creative Problem Solving Sourcebook*. Buffalo, N.Y.: Creative Education Foundation, 1987.

Pearlman, C. "Theoretical Model for Creativity." *Education*, 1983, *103*, 294–305.

Perkins, D. N. "Creativity by Design." *Educational Leadership*, Sept. 1984, pp. 18–25.

Piaget, J. *The Child and Reality*. New York: Penguin, 1976a.

Piaget, J. *To Understand Is to Invent: The Future of Education*. New York: Penguin, 1976b.

Porter, C. A., and Suefeld, P. "Integrative Complexity in the Correspondence of Literary Figures: Effects of Personal and Social Stress." *Journal of Personality and Social Psychology*, 1981, *40*, 321–330.

Puccio, G. J., Treffinger, D. J., and Talbot, R. "Exploratory Examination of Relations Between Creative Styles and Creative Products." *Creativity Research Journal*, 1995, *8*, 157–172.

Rank, O. *Art and Artists*. (C. F. Atkinson, trans.). New York: Knopf, 1932.

Reiter-Palmon, R., Mumford, M. D., Boes, J. O., and Runco, M. A. "Problem Construction and Creativity: The Role of Ability, Cue Consistency, and Active Processing." *Creativity Research Journal*, 1995.

Riccio, D. C., Rabinowitz, V. C., and Axelrod, S. "Memory: When Less Is More." *American Psychologist*, 1994, *49*, 917–926.

Richards, R. "How Normal Is the Creative Child?" Paper presented at the meeting of the American Psychological Association, Los Angeles, Aug. 1994.

Richards, R. *Everyday Creativity: Coping and Thriving in the 21st Century*. Unpublished manuscript, 1995.

Rickards, T., and De Cock, C. "Understanding Organizational Creativity: Toward a Multi-Paradigmatic Approach." In M. A. Runco (ed.), *Creativity Research Handbook,* Vol. 2. Cresskill, N.J.: Hampton Press, in press.

Rogers, C. "Toward a Theory of Creativity." In H. H. Anderson (ed.), *Creativity and Its Cultivation.* New York: HarperCollins, 1959.

Root-Bernstein, R. *Discovering.* Cambridge, Mass.: Harvard University Press, 1988.

Root-Bernstein, R. *Polymaths, Transformational Thinking, and the Creative Process.* Paper presented at the Chicago Academy of Sciences, Chicago, Oct. 1993.

Rosenblatt, E., and Winner, E. "The Art of Children's Drawings." *Journal of Aesthetic Education,* 1988, *22,* 3–15.

Rothenberg, A. "Creativity in Adolescence." *Psychoanalytic Clinics of North America,* 1990a, *13,* 415–434.

Rothenberg, A. "Creativity, Mental Health, and Alcoholism." *Creativity Research Journal,* 1990b, *3,* 179–201.

Rothenberg, A. "The Janusian Process in Scientific Creativity." *Creativity Research Journal,* in press.

Rothenberg, A., and Hausman, C. R. "Metaphor and Creativity." In M. A. Runco (ed.), *Creativity Research Handbook,* Vol. 1. Cresskill, N.J.: Hampton Press, in press.

Rubenson, D. L. "On Creativity, Economics, and Baseball." *Creativity Research Journal,* 1991, *3,* 205–209.

Rubenson, D. L., and Runco, M. A. "The Psychoeconomic Approach to Creativity." *New Ideas in Psychology,* 1992, *10,* 131–147.

Rubenson, D. E., and Runco, M. A. "The Psychoeconomic View of Creative Work in Groups and Organizations." *Creativity and Innovation Management,* 1995, *4.*

Runco, M. A. "Maximal Performance on Divergent Thinking Tests by Gifted, Talented, and Nongifted Children." *Psychology in the Schools,* 1986, *23,* 308–315.

Runco, M. A. "Children's Divergent Thinking and Creative Ideation." *Developmental Review,* 1992, *12,* 233–264.

Runco, M. A. "Moral Creativity: Intentional and Unconventional." *Creativity Research Journal,* 1993a, *6,* 17–28.

Runco, M. A. "Operant Theories of Insight, Originality, and Creativity." *American Behavioral Scientist,* 1993b, *37,* 59–74.

Runco, M. A. "Creativity and Its Discontents." In M. P. Shaw and M. A. Runco (eds.), *Creativity and Affect.* Norwood, N.J.: Ablex, 1994a.

Runco, M. A. *Problem Finding, Problem Solving, and Creativity.* Norwood, N.J.: Ablex, 1994b.

Runco, M. A. "Insight for Creativity, Expression for Impact." *Creativity Research Journal,* 1995, *8,* 377–390.

Runco, M. A. "Creativity Need Not Be Social." In A. Montuori and R. Purser (eds.), *Social Creativity,* Vol. 1. Cresskill, N.J.: Hampton Press, in press.

Runco, M. A., and Chand, I. "Problem Finding, Evaluative Thinking, and Creativity." In M. A. Runco (ed.), *Problem Finding, Problem Solving, and Creativity.* Norwood, N.J.: Ablex, 1994.

Runco, M. A., and Charles, R. "Developmental Trends in Creative Potential and Creative Performance." In M. A. Runco (ed.), *Creativity Research Handbook,* Vol. 1. Cresskill, N.J.: Hampton Press, in press.

Runco, M. A., Ebersole, P., and Mraz, W. "Self-Actualization and Creativity." *Journal of Social Behavior and Personality,* 1991, *6,* 161–167.

Runco, M. A., Johnson, D., and Gaynor, J. R. "The Judgmental Base of Creativity and Implications for the Study of Gifted Youth." In A. Fishkin, B. Cramond, and P. Olszewski-Kubilius (eds.), *Creativity in Youth: Research and Methods.* Cresskill, N.J.: Hampton Press, in press.

Runco, M. A., and Richards, R. (eds.). *Eminent Creativity, Everyday Creativity, and Health.* Norwood, N.J.: Ablex, in press.

Runco, M. A., and Sakamoto, S. O. "Optimization as a Guiding Principle in Research on Creative Problem Solving." In T. Helstrup, G. Kaufmann, and K. H. Teigen (eds.),

   Problem Solving and Cognitive Processes: Essays in Honor of Kjell Raaheim. London: Kingsley, 1996.

Russ, S. W. "Primary Process Thinking, Divergent Thinking, and Coping in Children." *Journal of Personality,* 1988, *52,* 539–548.

Sampson, E. E. "Cognitive Psychology as Ideology." *American Psychologist,* 1988, *36,* 730–743.

Schuldberg, D. "Giddiness and Horror in the Creative Process." In M. P. Shaw and M. A. Runco (eds.), *Creativity and Affect.* Norwood, N.J.: Ablex, 1994.

Schwebel, M. "Moral Creativity as Artistic Transformation." *Creativity Research Journal,* 1993, *6,* 65–81.

Shalley, C. E. "Effects of Productivity Goals, Creativity Goals, and Personal Discretion on Individual Creativity." *Journal of Personality and Social Psychology,* 1991, *76,* 179–185.

Sheldon, K. M. "Creativity and Goal Conflict." *Creativity Research Journal,* 1995, 8, 299–306.

Simonton, D. K. "Quality and Purpose, Quantity and Chance." *Creativity Research Journal,* 1988, *1,* 68–74.

Singer, D. G., and Singer, J. L. *The House of Make-Believe: Play and the Developing Imagination.* Cambridge, Mass.: Harvard University Press, 1990.

Smith, G.J.W., and Amner, G. "Creativity and Perception." In M. A. Runco (ed.), *Creativity Research Handbook,* Vol. 1. Cresskill, N.J.: Hampton Press, in press.

Smith, G.J.W., and Carlsson, I. "Creativity in Early and Middle School Years." *International Journal of Behavioral Development,* 1983, *6,* 167–195.

Sternberg, R. J., and Lubart, T. E. "The Role of Intelligence in Creativity." In M. A. Runco (ed.), *Critical Creative Processes.* Cresskill, N.J.: Hampton Press, in press.

Subotnik, R. "Factors from the Structure of Intellect Model Associated with Gifted Adolescents' Problem Finding in Science: Research with Westinghouse Science Talent Search Winners." *Journal of Creative Behavior,* 1988, *22,* 42–54.

Taylor, C. "Process vs. Product Creativity." In C. Taylor (ed.), *Widening Horizons in Creativity.* New York: Wiley, 1964.

Torrance, E. P. "A Longitudinal Examination of the Fourth-Grade Slump in Creativity." *Gifted Child Quarterly,* 1968, *12,* 195–199.

Torrance, E. P. "Talent Among Young Children Who Are Economically Disadvantaged or Culturally Different." In J. Smutny (ed.), *Taxonomies.* Cresskill, N.J.: Hampton Press, in press.

Wakefield, J. "Problem Finding and Empathy in Art." In M. A. Runco (ed.), *Problem Finding, Problem Solving, and Creativity.* Norwood, N. J.: Hampton Press, 1994.

Weber, R. "Toward a Language of Invention and Synthetic Thinking." *Creativity Research Journal,* in press.

Welsh, G. S. *Creativity and Intelligence: A Personality Approach.* Chapel Hill, N.C.: Institute for Research in Social Science, 1975.

Wolf, F. M., and Larson, G. L. "On Why Adolescent Formal Operators May Not Be Creative Thinkers." *Adolescence,* 1981, *26,* 346–348.

MARK A. RUNCO is professor of child development at California State University, Fullerton.

*The major creative processes in children are reviewed
with a focus on affective processes and children's play.*

Development of Creative Processes
in Children

Sandra W. Russ

The field of creativity has identified cognitive, affective, and personality processes that are important in the creative act. Individuals who are high on some of these dimensions of creative processes will have a higher likelihood of producing a creative product. There are a number of different possible profiles of creative individuals. In general, the processes that are predictive of creativity in adults are the same as those that predict creativity in children. Of course, children do not have the technical expertise or mastery of the knowledge base in a field necessary to make a truly creative contribution. However, children do have good and novel ideas and productions that are creative for their age group. They do engage in creative acts and creative problem solving. As Thurstone (1952) stated, even though a discovery may have already occurred, if it is new to the individual, then it is a creative act.

Theoretically, creative processes should be stable over time. For example, children who are open to emotion in fantasy in play should have a rich, affect-laden fantasy life as adults. This chapter will review the major processes in children that should be predictive of adult creativity, with a particular focus on affective processes and children's play.

Model of Affect and Creativity

Russ (1993) developed a model of affect and creativity that articulated the role of affective processes in creativity and the relationships among affective, cognitive, and personality processes. Different configurations of these processes occur in different creative individuals and, perhaps, in different domains of creativity. Figure 2.1 presents a summary of the model. There is good consensus in the literature about what cognitive and personality processes are involved in the creative act.

In this model of affect and creativity, the major cognitive abilities that emerge as unique to and important in the creative process are linked to specific affective processes and to global personality traits. In some cases, the personality traits are behavioral reflections of the underlying affective process. One assumption of this model is that these specific affective processes and personality traits facilitate cognitive abilities.

Cognitive Processes. Two major categories of cognitive processes important in creativity are divergent thinking and transformation abilities. Both of these processes were identified by Guilford (1968) as being important in and unique to creative problem solving. *Divergent thinking* is thinking that goes off in different directions. For example, a typical item on a divergent thinking test would be "how many uses for a brick can you think of?" Guilford thought that the key concept underlying divergent production abilities is variety. Divergent thinking involves free association, broad scanning ability, and fluidity of thinking. Divergent thinking has been found to be relatively independent of intelligence (Runco, 1991). *Transformation abilities* enable the individual to reorganize information and break out of old ways of thinking. They enable the individual to transform or revise known material into new patterns or configurations.

Other cognitive processes important but not unique to creative problem solving include sensitivity to problems and problem finding (Getzels and Csikszentmihalyi, 1976); task persistence and trying alternative problem solving approaches (Weisberg, 1988); breadth of knowledge and wide range of interests (Barron and Harrington, 1981); insight and synthesizing abilities (Sternberg, 1988); and evaluative ability (Guilford, 1950; Runco, 1991).

Personality Processes. Major research programs in the area of personality and creativity led to a consensus about which personality processes are found in creative individuals or relate to tests of creativity. Barron and Harrington (1981), in their review of the literature, concluded that major personality characteristics important in creativity are: tolerance of ambiguity, openness to experience, independence of judgment, unconventional values, curiosity, preference for challenge and complexity, self-confidence, risk taking, and intrinsic motivation. Many of these personality variables may be behavioral manifestations of underlying cognitive and affective processes.

Affective Processes. Russ (1993) identified the types of affective processes that have emerged from diverse theoretical and research literatures as important in creativity. Five affective processes emerged as related to or facilitative of creative thinking. Two broad affective processes are access to affect-laden thoughts and openness to affect states.

Access to affect-laden thoughts is the ability to think about thoughts and images that contain emotional content. Primary process thinking and affective fantasies in daydreams and in play are examples of this category. Thoughts involving emotional themes such as aggressive and sexual ideation illustrate this kind of blending of affect and cognition.

Figure 2.1. Affect and Creativity: A Model

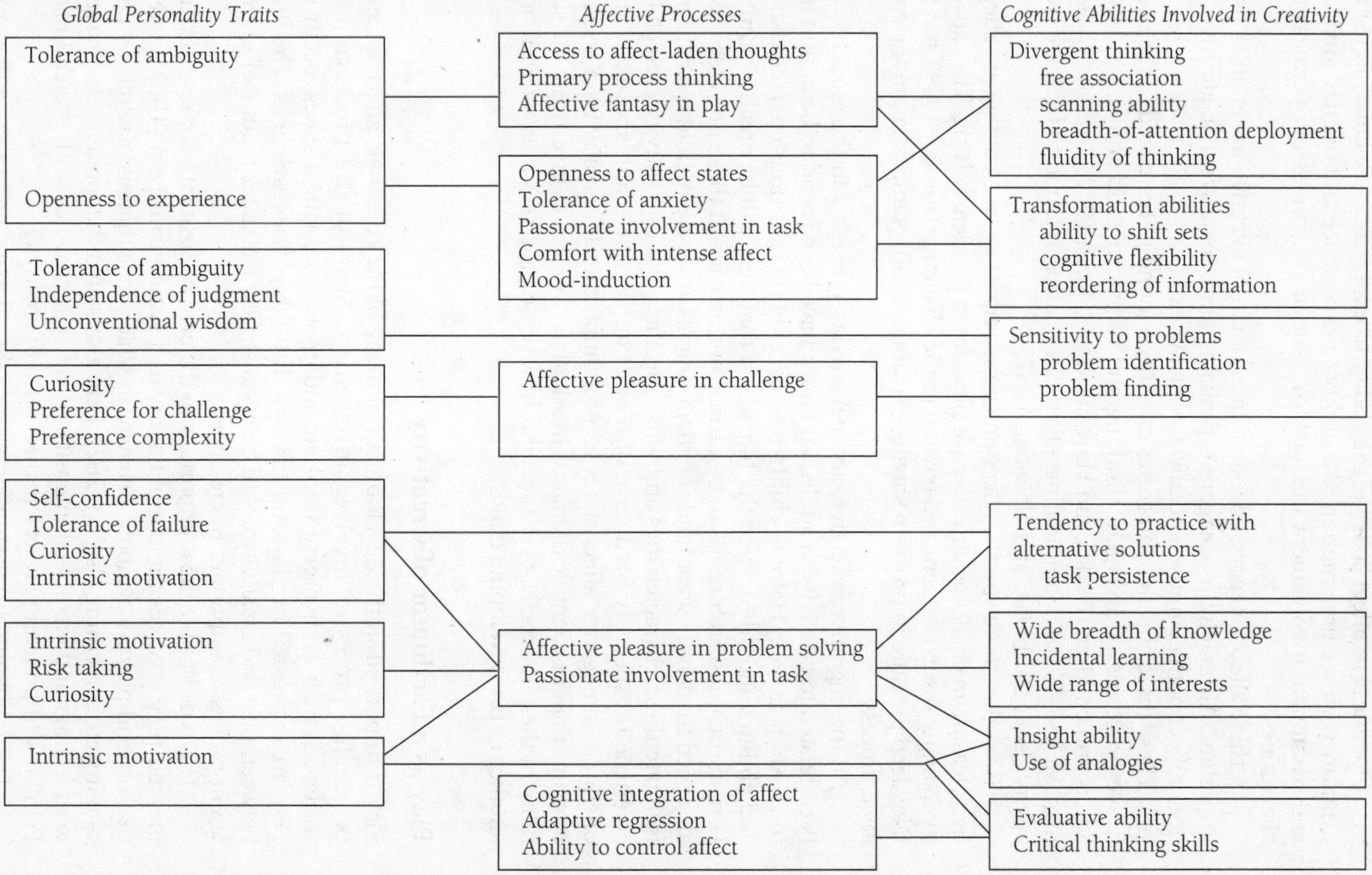

Global Personality Traits

- Tolerance of ambiguity
- Openness to experience
- Tolerance of ambiguity / Independence of judgment / Unconventional wisdom
- Curiosity / Preference for challenge / Preference complexity
- Self-confidence / Tolerance of failure / Curiosity / Intrinsic motivation
- Intrinsic motivation / Risk taking / Curiosity
- Intrinsic motivation

Affective Processes

- Access to affect-laden thoughts / Primary process thinking / Affective fantasy in play
- Openness to affect states / Tolerance of anxiety / Passionate involvement in task / Comfort with intense affect / Mood-induction
- Affective pleasure in challenge
- Affective pleasure in problem solving / Passionate involvement in task
- Cognitive integration of affect / Adaptive regression / Ability to control affect

Cognitive Abilities Involved in Creativity

- Divergent thinking / free association / scanning ability / breadth-of-attention deployment / fluidity of thinking
- Transformation abilities / ability to shift sets / cognitive flexibility / reordering of information
- Sensitivity to problems / problem identification / problem finding
- Tendency to practice with alternative solutions / task persistence
- Wide breadth of knowledge / Incidental learning / Wide range of interests
- Insight ability / Use of analogies
- Evaluative ability / Critical thinking skills

Openness to affect states is the ability to experience the emotion itself. Comfort with intense emotion, the ability to experience and tolerate anxiety, and passionate involvement in a task or issue are examples of openness to affect states.

A third affect category, cognitive integration of affective material, is also important. Although this category is probably more cognitive than affective, it does reflect both cognitive and affective elements.

These three affective categories have been found to be related to the cognitive processes of divergent thinking and transformation abilities in both adults and children (Dudek and Verreault, 1989; Russ, 1982; Russ and Grossman-McKee, 1990). Manipulating affect states has been found to facilitate creativity (Isen, Daubman, and Nowicki, 1987).

Two other more specific affect processes important in creativity are affective pleasure in challenge and affective pleasure in problem solving. The capacity to enjoy the excitement and tension in the challenge (Runco, 1994) and to take deep pleasure in problem solving (Amabile, 1990) is important in the creative process.

All the cognitive, affective, and personality processes in the model have been related to creativity in adults, and most have been found to be important in children as well. Helping children to develop these various characteristics and abilities should increase the likelihood that they will be creative adults. Longitudinal research needs to be carried out on each of these processes. We also need to identify what kinds of environments and parent-child interactions facilitate these characteristics and what specific types of creativity each characteristic is especially predictive of. For example, one might speculate that openness to negative affect states is more important for creativity in artistic domains than in scientific domains. In addition, we need to investigate the stability of these processes over time and how these processes interact with one another in the developing child.

Play as a Facilitator of Creativity

Play is important in the development of many of the cognitive, affective, and personality processes involved in creativity. Many of the processes just reviewed, such as divergent thinking and openness to affect states, occur in play, are expressed in play, and develop through play experiences. The link between play and creativity could be because play facilitates a number of different processes important in creativity.

The type of play most important to the area of creativity is pretend play. Pretend play involves the use of fantasy and symbolism. Fein (1987) stated that pretend play is a symbolic behavior in which "one thing is playfully treated as if it were something else" (p. 282). Fein also stated that pretense is charged with feelings and emotional intensity. Affect is intertwined with pretend play. Fein viewed pretend play as a natural form of creativity.

The following discussion focuses on the affective processes in play and the link between affect in play and creativity. For reviews of the literature that discuss all types of creative processes and play, see Singer and Singer (1990), Vandenberg, (1988), and Russ (in press *a*). The material presented here is drawn from the Russ (in press *a*) review of play and creativity.

Theories of Play, Affect, and Creativity. Slade and Wolf (1994) stressed the importance of studying play in both the development of cognitive structure and in the mastering of emotions. Historically, these two questions have been studied separately, usually by different theoretical and research traditions. Slade and Wolf felt that the cognitive and affective functions of play are intertwined. "Just as the development of cognitive structures may play an important role in the resolution of emotional conflict, so emotional consolidation may provide an impetus to cognitive advances and integration" (p. xv). They imply a working together of emotional functioning and cognitive structure. This working together could be especially important in creativity—access to emotions might alter developing cognitive structure and vice versa.

Fein (1987) viewed play as a natural form of creativity. She studied fifteen "master players" and concluded that good pretend play consisted of cognitive characteristics such as object substitutions and the manipulation of object representations and the affective characteristic of what she called affective relations. Affective relations are symbolic units that represent affective relationships such as fear of, love of, anger at. Fein proposed an affective symbol system that represents real or imagined experience at a general level. She stated that these affective units constitute affect-binding representational templates that store salient information about affect-laden events. The units are "manipulated, interpreted, coordinated and elaborated in a way that makes affective sense to the players" (p. 292). These affective units are a key part of pretend play. In fact, Fein viewed pretend play as symbolic behavior organized around emotional and motivational issues. Fein implied that this affective symbol system is especially important for creative thinking. She stated that divergent thinking abilities like daydreams, pretend play, or drawing can activate the affective symbol system. Fein's major conclusion was that creative processes cannot be studied independently of an affective symbol system, a system probably facilitated through pretend play.

Fein's conceptualization is consistent with the psychoanalytic concept of primary process and creativity. Primary process thinking was first conceptualized by Freud ([1915] 1958) as an early, primitive system of thought that was drive-laden and not subject to rules of logic or oriented to reality. Another way to view primary process thought is as affect-laden cognition. Russ (1987, 1993, in press *b*) proposed that primary process is a subtype of affect in cognition. Primary process content is material around which the child had experienced early intense feeling states (for example, oral, anal, or aggressive). Primary process content could be stored in the affect symbol system proposed by Fein. According to psychoanalytic theory, primary process thinking facilitates creativity (Kris, 1952). Children and adults who have controlled access to primary process thinking should have a broader range of associations and be better divergent thinkers than individuals with less access to primary process. Freud ([1926]

1959) suggested that repression of so-called dangerous drive-laden content leads to a more general intellectual restriction, predicting that individuals with less access to affect-laden cognitions would have fewer associations in general. Thus, children who are more expressive of and open to affective content would develop a richer, more complex store of affect-laden memories. This richer store of affect symbols and memories would facilitate divergent thinking and transformation abilities because it provides a broader range of associations and a more flexible manipulation of images and ideas.

Primary process content can be expressed in play. As Waelder (1933) has said, play is a "leave of absence from reality" (p. 222) and is a place to let primary process thinking occur. Play can be important in the development of primary process thought.

Fein's (1987) theory and primary process theory are also consistent with Bower's (1981) conceptualization of affect and memory processes (see Russ, 1993). The work on mood and memory suggests that the search process for associations is broadened by the involvement of emotion. Russ (1993) proposed that if primary process is thought of as mood-relevant cognition, then it could fit into a mood and memory theoretical framework. When stirred, primary process content could trigger a broad associative network. Primary process content was stored into the memory system when emotion was present. Access to this primary process content would activate emotion nodes and associations, thus broadening the search process.

Vygotsky ([1930] 1967) also thought that play facilitated creativity. In a recent translation and integration of Vygotsky's work, Smolucha (1992) stated that Vygotsky viewed creativity as a developmental process facilitated through play. Vygotsky stated "The child's play activity is not simply a recollection of past experience but a creative reworking that combines impressions and constructs forming new realities addressing the needs of the child" ([1930] 1967, p. 7). Through play, children develop *combinatory imagination,* the ability to combine elements of experience into new situations and new behaviors. Combinatory imagination is part of artistic and scientific creativity. By adolescence, play evolves into fantasy and imagination that combines with conceptual thinking. Imagination has two parts in the adolescent—objective imagination and subjective imagination. Subjective imagination includes emotion and serves the emotional life. Impulse and thinking are combined in the activity of creative thinking.

Research Evidence. A growing body of research has found a relationship between play and creativity. Most of the research has been correlational in nature. Singer and Singer (1976), in a review of the literature, concluded that the capacity for imaginative play is positively related to divergent thinking. Singer and Rummo (1973) found a relationship between play and divergent thinking in kindergarten children. Play was found to facilitate divergent thinking in preschool children by Dansky (1980).

Until recently, the research on play and creativity has focused on cognitive variables as the explanatory mechanisms underlying the relationship. The various theoretical explanations of affect in play and creativity are just beginning to be tested.

Lieberman's (1977) work supports a relationship between affect and divergent thinking. She focused on the variable of playfulness that included the affective components of spontaneity and joy. She found that playful kindergarten children did better on divergent thinking than nonplayful children. Singer and Singer (1990) reported that positive affect was related to imaginative play. Singer and Singer (1981) also found that preschoolers rated as high-imagination players showed significantly more themes of danger and power than children with low imagination.

I was especially interested in investigating affective dimensions of play and creativity in my research program. To do so, I developed the Affect in Play Scale (APS) to meet the need for a standardized measure of affect in pretend play (Russ, 1987; 1993). Play sessions are individually administered five-minute standardized puppet play sessions. The play task involves two neutral looking puppets, one boy and one girl, with three small blocks laid out on a table. The instructions are standardized and direct the children to play with the puppets any way they like for five minutes in a free-play period. The play task and instructions are unstructured enough that individual differences in the use of affect in pretend play can emerge. The APS is appropriate for children from six to ten years of age. The play session is videotaped so that coding can occur later.

The APS measures the amount and types of affective expression in children's pretend play. It also measures cognitive dimensions of the play, such as quality of fantasy and imagination. Conceptually, APS taps three dimensions of affect in fantasy: *affect states*—actual emotional experiencing through expression of feeling states; *affect-laden thoughts*—affective content themes that include emotional content themes and primary process themes; and *cognitive integration of affect*.

These three categories of affect are three of the five affective dimensions proposed to be important in the creative process (Russ, 1993). This conceptualization of affect and creativity guided the development of the scale. In addition, both Holt's "Scoring System for Primary Process on the Rorschach" (1977) and Singer's (1973) play scales were used as models for the development of the scale. Details of the instructions and scoring system for the APS can be found in Russ (1993).

The major affect scores for the scale are frequency of affect units expressed, variety of affect categories expressed (eleven possible categories), and intensity of affect expression. There are also global ratings (1–5 scale) for comfort, quality of fantasy, and imagination. An affective integration score combines frequency of affect and quality of fantasy.

Once the APS was constructed, pilot studies were carried out to ensure that the task was appropriate for young children and would result in adequate individual differences among normal school populations (Russ, Grossman-McKee, and Rutkin, 1984). By 1984, the basics of the task and scoring system were in place. Recent studies have resulted in refinement of the scoring criteria and a shortening of the play period from ten minutes to five minutes. Children who express a high frequency of affect in their play typically have the puppets playing competitive games, fighting with each other, having fun together, eating (oral content), and expressing affection.

Affect in Play Scale and Creativity. To date, we have carried out nine validity studies with the APS. In each study, we obtained interrater reliabilities on fifteen or twenty subjects. Interrater reliabilities have been good, usually in the .80s and .90s, using a variety of different raters. We also obtained split-half reliability for frequency of affective expression comparing the second and fourth minutes with the third and fifth minutes. We found a split-half reliability of .85, which is very adequate (Russ and Peterson, 1990; Russ, 1993).

Two types of validating criteria have been used. One body of studies investigated affect in play and creativity. A second line of studies, not reviewed here, investigated play in the context of coping and adjustment (see D'Angelo, 1995; Russ, 1995).

The first study in the affect and creativity area (Russ and Grossman-McKee, 1990) investigated the relationships among the APS, divergent thinking, and primary process thinking on the Rorschach in sixty first- and second-grade children. As predicted, affective expression in play was significantly and positively related to divergent thinking, as measured by the Alternate Uses Test. All major scores on the APS were significantly correlated with divergent thinking, with correlations ranging from .23 ($p < .05$) between comfort and divergent thinking to .42 ($p < .001$) between frequency of affective expression and divergent thinking. All correlations remained significant when IQ was partialed out, because IQ had such low correlations with the APS. The lack of relationship between intelligence and any of the play scores is consistent with the theoretical model for the development of the scale and is similar to the results of Singer (1973). Also, there were no gender differences in the pattern of correlations between the APS and divergent thinking. We did find a relationship between the amount of primary process thinking on the Rorschach and the APS scores. Children who had more primary process responses on the Rorschach had more primary process in their play, had more affect in their play, and had higher fantasy scores than children with less primary process on the Rorschach. This is an important finding because it shows consistency in the construct of affective expression across two different types of situations.

The finding of a relationship between affect in play and divergent thinking (Russ and Grossman-McKee, 1990) was replicated by Russ and Peterson (1990), who used a larger sample of 121 first and second grade children. Once again, all the APS scores were significantly and positively related to the Alternate Uses Test, independent of intelligence. Again, there were no gender differences in the correlations. Thus, with this replication, we can have more confidence in the robustness of the finding of a relationship between affect in pretend play and creativity in young children. Children who have more access to emotion-laden fantasy and who can express emotion in play are more creative on divergent thinking tasks.

An important question about the APS is whether it is indeed measuring two separate dimensions of play—an affective dimension and a cognitive dimension—or is measuring one dimension—an affect in fantasy dimension. The results of two separate factor analyses with the scale suggest two separate dimensions. In Russ and Peterson's study, a factor analysis of the total sample was carried out using the principal component analysis with oblique rotation. An oblique solution yielded two separate factors as the best solution. The first and dominant dimension appeared to be cognitive. Imagination, organization, quality of fantasy, and comfort loaded on this first dimension. The second factor appeared to be affective. Frequency of affective expression, variety of affect categories, and intensity of affect loaded on this second factor. The factors, while separate, shared a significant amount of shared variance ($r = .76$).

A recent study by D'Angelo (1995) replicated the finding of two factors, one cognitive and one affective, with a sample of ninety-five first-, second-, and third-grade children. Another interesting finding by D'Angelo (1995) was a significant relationship between the APS and Singer's (1973) imaginative play predisposition interview. Good players in the APS reported that they prefer activities that require using imagination.

Stability of Dimensions of Play, Affect, and Creativity. A recent study (Russ, Robins, and Christiano, 1995) followed up the first and second graders in the Russ and Peterson (1990) study who were now fifth and sixth graders. This was a longitudinal study that explored the ability of the APS to predict creativity over a four-year period (five years in some cases because the study took two years to complete). Thirty-one children agreed to participate in the follow-up. The major finding was that quality of fantasy and imagination on the APS predicted divergent thinking over a four-year period (with values for $r = .34$ and $.42$, respectively; $p = < .05$ and $.01$). The correlation between variety of affect and divergent thinking was .25 but did not reach significance, possibly due to the small sample size. We also administered an adapted version of the play task to the older children with instructions "to put on a play with the puppets." We then scored the task based on the scoring criteria for the APS. Raters were blind to the earlier scores.

We found good stability in the dimensions being measured by the APS. For example, the size of the correlation between the two frequency of affect scores was .33 ($p < .05$); between the two variety of affect scores .38 ($p < .05$); and between the two frequency of positive affect scores .51 ($p < .01$). These correlations were for two scores separated by five years. Children who expressed more affect and better fantasy in play as first and second graders had more affect and better plays as sixth and seventh graders. In general, the size of the correlations is excellent for a period of four and five years and supports enduring, stable constructs of affective expression in fantasy that are predictive of creative thinking over time. These findings also suggest an enduring quality to the affective and cognitive dimensions of the APS over a five-year period.

These findings are consistent with those of Hutt and Bhavnani (1972), who found that creative inventiveness in preschool play related to later divergent thinking. Clark, Griffing, and Johnson (1989) also found a relationship between divergent thinking and play in preschoolers that was predictive of divergent thinking over a three-year period.

In addition to testing the longitudinal stability of the play scale scores, we also tested the stability of the Alternate Uses scores over the 4 years. Both the fluency scores and the flexibility scores were significantly positively correlated over time ($r = .30, p < .05; r = .46, p < .01$, respectively). It is noteworthy that the Alternate Uses test was individually administered to the first and second graders but group administered when these children were older. Despite the possible introduction of variance, the correlations further attest to the stability of divergent thinking abilities. We hope to follow these children into adolescence to see if these processes remain stable.

Concluding Comments

Children's fantasy play is an important activity in childhood because play facilitates so many of the cognitive and affective processes important in creativity. Pretend play helps children practice with divergent thinking (Singer and Singer, 1990), practice with symbol substitution, express and experience positive and negative affect, express and think about affect themes, resolve conflicts, and develop personality process such as curiosity, risk taking, and openness to experience. Developing programs that help children learn to play, such as those developed by Smilansky (1968), would be a good investment in the creative futures of our children. In addition, we need to determine the optimal environments for facilitating all the processes important in creativity. We also need to explore how these creative processes interact with other processes important for areas of child development such as social skills and values.

Systematic longitudinal research is an important research direction for the future. It would be useful to develop a battery of tests of creative processes in children and carry out longitudinal studies. Any model of creativity could be tested in this way. A battery of tests that would test Russ's (1993) model would include measures of affective processes such as affect-laden fantasy in play, personality processes such as openness to experience and self-confidence, and cognitive processes such as divergent thinking and problem identification. Then we could test the predictive power of the test battery for predicting actual creativity over time. However, the prediction of major creativity in adulthood may involve more than tapping necessary creative processes within the individual. Factors such as marginality, a driving and evolving passion, life circumstances, social context, and serendipity are crucial ingredients as well. True creativity may be more than the sum of the creative parts.

References

Amabile, T. "Within You, Without You: The Social Psychology of Creativity and Beyond." In M. A. Runco and R. S. Albert (eds.), *Theories of Creativity*. Thousand Oaks, Calif.: Sage, 1990.

Barron, F., and Harrington, D. "Creativity, Intelligence, and Personality." In M. Rosenzweig and L. Porter (eds.), *Annual Review of Psychology*, Vol. 32. Palo Alto, Calif.: Annual Reviews, 1981.

Bower, G. H. "Mood and Memory." *American Psychologist*, 1981, *36*, 129–148.

Clark, P., Griffing, P., and Johnson, L. "Symbolic Play and Ideational Fluency as Aspects of the Evolving Divergent Cognitive Style in Young Children." *Early Child Development and Care*, 1989, *51*, 77–88.

D'Angelo, L. "Child's Play: The Relationship Between the Use of Play and Adjustment Styles." Unpublished doctoral dissertation, Case Western Reserve University, Cleveland, Ohio, 1995.

Dansky, J. "Make Believe: A Mediator of the Relationship Between Play and Associative Fluency." *Child Development*, 1980, *51*, 576–579.

Dudek, S., and Verreault, R. "The Creative Thinking and Ego Functioning of Children." *Creativity Research Journal*, 1989, *2*, 64–86.

Fein, G. "Pretend Play: Creativity and Consciousness." In P. Gorlitz and J. Wohlwill (eds.), *Curiosity, Imagination, and Play*. Hillsdale, N.J.: Erlbaum, 1987.

Freud, S. "The Unconscious." In J. Strachey (ed. and trans.), *The Standard Edition of the Complete Psychological Works of Sigmund Freud*, Vol. 14. London: Hogarth Press, 1958. (Originally published 1915.)

Freud, S. "Inhibition, Symptoms, and Anxiety." In J. Strachey (ed. and trans.), *The Standard Edition of the Complete Psychological Works of Sigmund Freud*, Vol. 20. London: Hogarth Press, 1959. (Originally published 1926.)

Getzels, S., and Csikszentmihalyi, M. *The Creative Vision: A Longitudinal Study of Problem Finding in Art*. Somerset, N.J.: Wiley-Interscience, 1976.

Guilford, J. P. "Creativity." *American Psychologist*, 1950, *5*, 444–454.

Guilford, J. P. *Intelligence, Creativity and Their Educational Implications*. San Diego: Knapp, 1968.

Holt, R. R. "A Method for Assessing Primary Process Manifestations and Their Control in Rorschach Responses." In M. Rickers-Ovsiankina (ed.), *Rorschach Psychology*. New York: Krieger, 1977.

Hutt, C., and Bhavnani, R. "Predictions for Play." *Nature*, 1972, *237*, 171–172.

Isen, A., Daubman, K., and Nowicki, G. "Positive Affect Facilitates Creative Problem Solving." *Journal of Personality and Social Psychology*, 1987, *52*, 1122–1131.

Kris, E. *Psychoanalytic Explorations in Art*. Madison, Conn.: International Universities Press, 1952.

Lieberman, J. N. *Playfulness: Its Relationship to Imagination and Creativity*. New York: Academic Press, 1977.

Runco, M. A. *Divergent Thinking*. Norwood, N.J.: Ablex, 1991.

Runco, M. A. "Creativity and Its Discontents." In M. P. Shaw and M. A. Runco (eds.), *Creativity and Affect*. Norwood, N.J.: Ablex, 1994.

Russ, S. "Sex Differences in Primary Process Thinking and Flexibility in Problem Solving in Children." *Journal of Personality Assessment*, 1982, *45*, 569–577.

Russ, S. "Assessment of Cognitive Affective Interaction in Children: Creativity, Fantasy, and Play Research." In J. Butcher and C. Spielberger (eds.), *Advances in Personality Assessment*, Vol. 6. Hillsdale, N.J.: Erlbaum, 1987.

Russ, S. *Affect and Creativity: The Role of Affect and Play in the Creative Process*. Hillsdale, N.J.: Erlbaum, 1993.

Russ, S. "Creativity and Play." In M. A. Runco (ed.), *Creativity Research Handbook*, Vol. 3. Cresskill, N.J.: Hampton Press, in press *a*.

Russ, S. "Psychoanalytic Theory and Creativity: Cognition and Affect Revisited." In J. Masling and R. Borstein (eds.), *Psychoanalysis as Developmental Psychology,* Vol. 6. Washington D.C.: APA Books, in press *b.*

Russ, S., and Grossman-McKee, A. "Affective Expression in Children's Fantasy Play, Primary Process Thinking on the Rorschach, and Divergent Thinking." *Journal of Personality Assessment,* 1990, *54,* 756–771.

Russ, S., Grossman-McKee, A., and Rutkin, Z. Affect in Play Scale: Pilot Project. Unpublished raw data, 1984.

Russ, S., and Peterson, N. "The Affect in Play Scale: Predicting Creativity and Coping in Children." Unpublished manuscript, 1990.

Russ, S., Robins, D., and Christiano, B. "The Affect in Play Scale: Longitudinal Prediction." Paper presented at the meeting of the Society for Personality Assessment, Atlanta, Mar. 1995.

Singer, D. G., and Singer, J. L. *The House of Make-Believe: Play and the Developing Imagination.* Cambridge, Mass.: Harvard University Press, 1990.

Singer, D. L., and Rummo, J. "Ideation Creativity and Behavioral Style in Kindergarten Age Children." *Developmental Psychology,* 1973, *8,* 154–161.

Singer, J. L. *Child's World of Make-Believe.* New York: Academic Press, 1973.

Singer, J. L., and Singer, D. L. "Imaginative Play and Pretending in Early Childhood: Some Experimental Approaches." In A. Davids (ed.), *Child Personality and Psychopathology,* Vol. 3. New York: Wiley, 1976.

Singer, J. L., and Singer, D. L. *Television, Imagination, and Aggression.* Hillsdale, N.J.: Erlbaum, 1981.

Slade, A., and Wolf, D. *Children at Play.* New York: Oxford University Press, 1994.

Smilansky, S. *The Effects of Sociodramatic Play on Disadvantaged Preschool Children.* New York: Wiley, 1968.

Smolucha, F. "A Reconstruction of Vygotsky's Theory of Creativity." *Creative Research Journal,* 1992, *5,* 49–67.

Sternberg, R. "A Three-Facet Model of Creativity." In R. J. Sternberg (ed.), *The Nature of Creativity.* New York: Cambridge University Press, 1988.

Thurstone, L. "Creative Talent." In L. Thurstone (ed.), *Applications of Psychology.* New York: HarperCollins, 1952.

Vandenberg, B. "The Realities of Play." In D. Morrison (ed.), *Organizing Early Experience: Imagination and Cognition in Childhood.* Amityville, N.Y.: Baywood, 1988.

Vygotsky, L. S. *Vaobraszeniye i tvorchestvo v deskom voraste* [Imagination and creativity in childhood]. Moscow: Prosvescheniye, 1967. (Originally published 1930.)

Waelder, R. "Psychoanalytic Theory of Play." *Psychoanalytic Quarterly,* 1933, *2,* 208–224.

Weisberg, R. "Problem Solving and Creativity." In R. J. Sternberg (ed.), *The Nature of Creativity.* New York: Cambridge University Press, 1988.

SANDRA W. RUSS is professor of psychology and chair of the Psychology Department at Case Western Reserve University, Cleveland, Ohio.

We generally overestimate the ease and naturalness of the development of creativity in childhood and, even more so, past it.

Some Reasons Why Childhood Creativity Often Fails to Make It Past Puberty into the Real World

Robert S. Albert

Long before puberty, when the major cognitive changes of adolescence are expected, the child's orientation to and mode of handling novelty, loss, and distinct breaks (gaps) in the continuity of experience (personal and impersonal) are well formed and operate without much conscious prodding. This orientation precedes and directs whatever giftedness or talents may appear during childhood and later. And although I am speaking as much about the noncognitive orientation to self and experience as about some cognitive capacities, I believe that understanding the source and formulating this orientation helps explain two developmental outcomes: that giftedness and talent alone do not lead to creativeness, and that in general what the individual is in this regard prior to adolescence is predictive of how (and even why) the cognitive and social changes of adolescence will be incorporated into his or her continuous development and experience. The evidence for this and the factors that need explaining are as follows.

Over the years I have been impressed by six sets of data in the literature on giftedness and creativity. When taken together, I believe they argue that there is little research evidence or reason for believing that the type and level of creativity we see in childhood are likely to become the type and level of creativity one can observe after puberty among adolescents and adults.

Now, the six observations.

I wish to thank the Arthur D. and Catherine T. MacArthur Foundation for its support in the preparation of this chapter.

How very different the creativity seen in childhood is from the creativity seen among some adolescents and adults. There is a two-part corollary to this. The first part says that there are few creative and gifted children and adolescents who become noticeably creative as adults, and the second says that childhood creativity only poorly predicts adult, real-world creativity.

How weak a role much of a child's education has in the development of creativity. Indeed, education regularly inhibits the transformation of early giftedness and talent into creativity; this is especially evident in the nonmathematical and nonscientific domains and in the formal (and conventional) instruction during the ages up to eleven years, just prior to puberty. This observation relates to the next one.

Holding aside questions of heredity and constitution, how significant to the development and application of real-world, adult creativity are a limited number of noncognitive variables and facilitating experiences. These work first within the family and progressively widen out into selected parts of the child's social and cultural environments. This observation alerts us to influences of informal education and immersion in a self-selected program of informal education by a gifted and talented adolescent.

How obvious and powerful are the differences between the families of notably creative eminent persons and those of persons far less creative who nonetheless become eminent through the institutional and social positions they hold. It is of equal importance to note how early these differences begin to influence a child's creative potential.

How early one can see the beginning of what can be called an individual's creative orientation. This *creative orientation* is determined by specific characteristics within the family (such as socioeconomic status), particular cognitive characteristics of the parents (such as their degree of intellectuality and reflectiveness), and the quality and consistency of the individual's relationships with each of the parents (for example, supportive, indifferent, overly involved).

How important for the development of adult, real-world creativity are the changes a child undergoes at puberty and afterward. It is useful to assess these changes in terms of the child's cognitive, emotional, and social maturity, and to note how these relate to adolescent and child interests and creative abilities.

When put together, these observations tell us that not all children, gifted or not, are creative and that the majority of those who do show early creative potential will not show substantial creativity after puberty into adolescence or adulthood. Furthermore, because the subjects these observations and research are based upon are adolescents or older, two rather distressing conclusions present themselves. The first is that the creativity one sees after puberty is not an extension or variation of the creativity one sees earlier among younger subjects; the two result from fairly distinct developmental conditions and pathways. The second relates to the assertion one sometimes reads that it is primarily the cognitive changes ushered in after puberty that make so-called real, mature creativity possible, the implication being that this is the period when special training and encouragement in creativity capitalize on these changes and are most effective. But as the evidence shows, such training and special instructions often seem to do little good. The effort seems to be generally irrelevant and ineffective in regard to creativity itself—even though there is also evidence that training aimed at creativity may enhance academic achievement (Cutrona and others, 1994; Feldhusen, 1991). This doesn't mean that earlier experiences and abilities do not matter in regard to creativity—they do, but in other less direct ways after puberty (Kubie, 1958).

Background

The break in creativity seen in childhood and after puberty is well documented (Hedges and Nowell, 1995; Siegler and Kotovsky, 1993). What is not always noted is that while childhood creativity is often limited to play and school activities, the creativity found among some adolescents and adults shows a minimal degree of continuity from childhood into adolescence and adulthood. This raises the question of whether or not the creativity of those children that does not go past puberty is basically different from that of those children who are creative in adolescence and often well into adulthood.

Over the years, a variety of reasons have been suggested for this shortfall, most of which center on families and their interface with schools and society. Usually in such explanations there is something quite different found among these families that helps to explain some of the differences between the highly creative and much less creative individual (see Albert, 1994a, 1994b, 1994c; Goertzel and Goertzel, 1962; Ludwig, 1994; MacKinnon, 1978, 1993). Unfortunately, their subjects are all adolescents or older and well into their developments (Albert, 1994b; Albert and Runco, 1987; Getzels and Jackson, 1962, Helson, 1985).

One of the lessons one learns from these studies is how subjects and their families are performing late in their development. Moreover, several assumptions are often made in such research: that the differences have always existed as we find them, and that in all probability they will continue with little change. True as this may be, it still leaves unanswered the questions of when and why these distinctive family-child systems first began to function as they do in regard to creativity.

In trying to explain the sources of creative potential, it would be best to look for the earliest parent-child experience nearly every parent and child has to meet and go through. Along with the obvious methodological reasons for this, there is an existential reason. Parents' and infants' earliest interactions are for the purpose of survival, regardless of the family's particular situation and resources. How this is done can vary, but the interactions that work best are not fixed, rigid, or impersonal; in most instances, they qualify as adaptive. Creative behaviors are the core of human adaptation (Albert, in press). Long before a child's giftedness, talent, or skills become apparent, parental views of the world and beliefs about what it takes to succeed (survive) determines what the parents believe is necessary for the child to learn and do well at. These considerations determine a major proportion of the parents' parenting style and goals.

Along with a wealth of empirical studies, there are three earlier conceptual arguments for this chapter's approach to creativity. Probably the earliest discussion of parent-child separation relevant to creativity is Freud's ([1900] 1953) *The Interpretation of Dreams*. Writing soon after the death of his father, Freud discusses their relationship and his dreams about his father. A later and more explicit discussion is found in Winnicott (1971, 1976), and a third suggestion is in attachment theory (and research), with its emphasis on the essential role of early attachment in survival, and how attachments often foster an infant's ever-widening explorations (Ainsworth, 1973; Keller and Boigs, 1991; Winnicott, 1976). In my search for the earliest ubiquitous experience demanding parental and child adaptation, I turned to something often seen in the developmental histories of a surprisingly large proportion of eminent men and women.

I have long been intrigued by the disproportionately high numbers of creative, eminent men and women who experience parent-loss before adolescence (Albert, 1971, 1980, 1994b; Berrington, 1983; Edel, 1975; Helson, 1978; Ludwig, 1994; Martindale, 1972). Of course, such a loss does not appear in every eminent person's history, nor does eminence always depend upon creativity (Albert, 1994c); nevertheless, early losses are frequent enough among the creative to take seriously. Reviewing the literature on eminent and creative persons, loss and bereavement, and other types of separation (Amato and Keith, 1991; Cleiver, 1993; Fergusson, Lynskey, and Horwood, 1994; Lund, Caserta, and Dimond, 1993; Sanders, 1993; Shepard and Barrclough, 1976; Silverman and Worden, 1993), I found that the way most bereaved persons of all ages cope with their loss differs from the way people tend to handle divorce, sporadic separations, or abandonment by a living parent. The research shows that at least in Western cultures, the bereaved—from the earliest moments of loss— make deliberate efforts to stay in contact with the deceased. Furthermore, though this can differ with the bereaved's age, ranging from activities like cherishing a picture or possession of the deceased to maintaining the subtlest memories, their effort is lifelong and contact is rarely lost. This leads us to that important clue into the first conditions for creativity within the infant and child's experiences of separation and loss, and how they are adapted to. Quite simply, an infant's and young child's response to separation and loss can be their prototypical creative experience.

The Earliest Creation of Transitional Objects

If separation is the prototypical experience in which creativity may develop, then the earliest creative product would be the transitional objects a young child creates to moderate the anxieties and uncertainties in this situation and as a bridge from known to unknown (Winnicott, 1971, 1976). Part of the power of transitional objects is their highly personal nature; as Winnicott pointed out, only the child can create them. What gives them their early importance is that object-permanence can occur as early as three to four months of age (Baillargeon and DeVos, 1991). Nonetheless, a transitional object's significance is less in the age it is created and more in its symbolic power to bridge the gap between the known and unknown. Just as in the range of efforts a bereaved person might use to cope with death, there is no item best suited to become a transitional object—its significance must be created by the child. Literally anything may become a transitional object, from a smelly doll to a long-held memory, as Citizen Kane's sled "Rosebud" shows us. What matters most is that because the transitional object's basic purpose is to modify the acute stresses and confusions of separation as the child experiences them, the child has a strong incentive to accept the structure built on the object and thus to trust his or her own rudimentary creativity—whether or not anyone else accepts it. If people caring for a child can accept this early personal initiative, even knowing it might not be as protective as they are, then the child's creativity has a better chance to continue.

This sequence tells us something important about creativity in general. Just as another person cannot designate or offer a transitional object to a child, the child, like any creative person, must initiate this creative process from within. However, another person can deny, resist, or denigrate the creation and use of transitional objects, and hinder the further development of creativity. As we all know, it is never a sure thing that creativity will continue to develop, and early creativity's continuation depends largely upon a family's reaction to it.

It is no coincidence that among the relatively few observed personality dispositions often credited to highly creative persons are the high need for autonomy, especially in creative work, and the capacity to work alone. Both of these begin their development in childhood (Albert and Runco, 1989) and bear on later issues of identity and decision making (Waterman and Waterman, 1974). Losses and uncertainties are not unique to creative persons, and those adolescents who have, prior to adolescence, learned to experience loss and novelty in their early separation experiences without denying or ignoring them should have greater possibilities of becoming creative than those who have learned to deny and to avoid such experiences. One reason for this is the core to dealing with those situations that must be confronted is creativity as well as loss.

For decades—from Barron (1953) up to Loewenstein (1994)—studies have shown that the capacity to acknowledge and experience "gaps" (to denote complexity and novelty) is a principal personality disposition favoring curiosity and creative behavior. Regardless of the field and domain involved, the common cognitive experience required of creative persons is their capacity to experience and resolve gaps, novelty, and curiosity through exploration for new information and order, whether in the crib or the laboratory. Because of the relationships of gaps, curiosity, and creativity to each other and to exploration, I want to go into their developments.

Gaps, Novelty, Curiosity, and Exploration

Curiosity and exploration are the interrelated results of cognitive development. Both can be seen active as early as infancy; usually if you have one, you almost certainly have the beginning of the other. And as already suggested, curiosity and exploration are related developmentally insofar as they are both influenced by the child's separations and attachments (Ainsworth, 1973; Bowlby 1973; Keller and Boigs, 1991).

There is, however, one important developmental difference between curiosity and exploration. Exploration appears earliest in the course of an infant's interactions with the environment. This can be seen in the newborn's orienting response, which becomes progressively directed under the baby's control. Afterward and well within the first year, for the average healthy baby, curiosity comes into operation as a motivational state. This development is doubly significant because it signifies the presence and awareness of a self (Stern, 1985), which in turn becomes a basis of exploratory behavior. What makes the development of a self and self-awareness so powerful is that the self, the experience of curiosity, and exploration in the service of both can form an increasingly complex Piagetian feedback system. Just as curiosity can lead to exploration, exploration can satisfy (relieve) and even increase one's curiosity; together they can lead to a complex sense of self and expectations powering creative behavior (see Hull, 1988, on the importance of curiosity as a major motivation of creative scientists).

Puberty as a Development Marker

One's age, especially early in life, is at best an approximate marker for one's degree of maturation. This is nowhere more evident than in the areas of cognitive-ego development (Loevinger and Wessler, 1970; Piaget, 1952) and psychosocial development (Erikson, 1959). In all cases, there is a rough chronology to these developments agreed upon, but no agreement on the ages at which clear transitions from less mature to later more mature functions will appear. Kagan (1971) proposed that our most reliable and clearest sign for maturation is when biological changes take place. These are not only obvious but they signal that a child is prepared for newer and qualitatively different experiences.

The most significant period of maturation in the development of creativity is puberty. It usually ushers in not only bodily changes but new cognitive, emotional, and social competencies as well. There should be little doubt that maturation plays an important role in creativity. The biological changes of puberty are not our only clear signs of maturation, but a number of the changes they mark are important for creativity.

I see the inhibiting and facilitating influence of level of maturity in creativity and achievement in several ways. One example is the use of denial as a defense, which MacKinnon (1978) found to be antagonistic to creativity and intellectualizing as a coping mechanism (Haan, 1963; Vaillant, 1977; Vaillant, Bond, and Vaillant, 1985) especially if there is the more abstract symbolic cognitive process expected after puberty (Case, 1978; Piaget, 1952; Raz-Kohen, 1977; Siegler, 1986). Perhaps the most convincing evidence of maturation's role in high, often eminent achievement is the remarkably consistent timetable for first major creative products and exceptional sports performances, almost all of which appear in the early to middle twenties in a variety of domains and across cultures (Albert, 1975, 1990, 1994b, 1994c; Raskin, 1936).

Cognitive Maturity and the Ego Defenses

The preceding discussion is weighted toward conditions when things go well, in which case maturation and development, among other things, are sources of creative possibilities. But what happens when early separations, instead of being taken as opportunities to experience gaps and to explore them, are ignored—or worse, denied and invalidated? Both ego defenses and coping mechanisms become powerful antecedents to a person's perspective on life, and therefore, they do more than offer protection. They go far into the construction of the sense of self and the kind of world it exists in. And this has a great impact on the levels of cognitive maturity and complexity that can be reached.

Although professional interest in defense mechanisms has a long history (Freud, 1936; Freud, [1894] 1966), it is surprising to find how limited the empirical (as contrasted to clinical) information is regarding the developmental chronology of ego defenses (see Bond, Gardiner, and Sigal, 1983; Brody, Rozek, and Muten, 1985; Cramer, 1991; Haan, 1963, 1977; Levit, 1993; Miller and Swanson, 1960; Smith and Danielson, 1982; Smith and Carlsson, 1983, 1990; Swanson, 1961, 1988; Vaillant, 1977; Vaillant, Bond, and Vaillant, 1985; and Weinstock, 1967, for reviews and data). The few studies devoted to specific ages and defenses are discussed by Cramer (1991), Haan (1977), Jacobson and others, (1986), Levit (1993), and Swanson (1988).

Because all ego defenses, with the possible exceptions of intellectualization and sublimation, defend through distorting, repressing, and depersonalizing one's experience, it is easy to see how they resist and often corrupt the development and subsequent exercise of creative behavior (MacKinnon, 1978; Smith and Carlsson, 1990; Vaillant, 1977). To summarize the evidence: The earlier in development the defenses function, the more likely they are to block, distort, or at least inhibit a child—gifted or not—from acquiring the personal orientation and skills needed to become creative.

Just how early can this inhibition occur? A search in the literature on defenses shows that primitive efforts at denial often appear in infancy and denial as an ego defense can be reliably observed by age four. On the other hand, the coping mechanism, the intellectualizing that supports creativity as much as denial prevents it, must await the presence of those cognitive changes taking place after puberty (Piaget, 1952; Siegler, 1986). There are good reasons for understanding the similarities and differences between ego defense mechanisms and creativity, especially when it is argued by some (Freud, [1900] 1953; Jacobson and others, 1986; Vaillant, 1977) that creativity is itself a (sophisticated) defense or that the adolescent defense of intellectualization enhances creativity in the face of contesting empirical evidence (Cramer, 1991; Haan, 1963, 1977).

The most obvious similarity between ego defenses and creativity is that they are basically control mechanisms used to maintain homeostasis against threatening or overwhelming tension, cognitive disorder, and meaninglessness. This similarly tells us that ego defenses and creativity usually operate in similar situations—threatening, unpredicted, and novel situations. Therefore, the cognitive goal of ego defenses and creativity is similar—to reduce discontinuities, gaps, and high degrees of novelty to the point where they become sensible, manageable, and predictable. Perhaps the most significant difference between ego defenses and creativity, and the source of their particular influences in cognitive development, is their use of information. Whereas ego defenses distort, repress, and close off many sources of information inside and around the individual, creativity lives on information. The creative person (at any age) seeks, explores, and synthesizes information from inner and outside sources. Pulling together the similarities and differences, it seems that ego defenses and creativity each set in motion very different approaches to locating and the use of information.

Experimental evidence demonstrating that preadolescents' level of cognitive maturity and defense mechanisms are significantly associated with their interest in and capacity for creativity appears in Cramer (1991), Crandall and Battle (1970), Smith and Carlsson (1983), and indirectly in Getzels and Jackson (1962) and Swanson (1988). To different degrees, this research is directly concerned with the connections among subjects' age, their methods of handling anxiety, and their complexity of demonstrated creativity. To conserve space, I'll focus on Smith's research. He and his coworkers find that creative children—especially ages ten to thirteen years—and some adults, unlike less creative subjects, are able to use moderate anxiety as a signal, alerting them that their thresholds between danger and safety are about to be crossed. Often this signal is "an indication that a contradiction (gap?) is about to reach awareness requiring [sic] to be dealt with in a constructive way by the creative subject" (Smith and Danielson, 1982, pp. 191–192). More recently, Smith and Carlsson (1990) have emphasized the importance of intentionality in creative behavior as a function of subjects' maturity, to say nothing of their low to moderate defenses. After several decades of experimental research with nonclinical subjects from age five into middle age, Smith and Carlsson (1990, p. 130) drew a very important conclusion about the importance of age, especially the years just before puberty, for creativity. Their conclusion was that although the "attempts at creativity activity in preschoolers [are] more or less premature and accidental, even if charmingly disrespectful of adult conventions . . . that [it is] at age 10–11 we enter the first stage of true creativity." And not all children reached this stage.

The reader might have the impression that creativity is only involved in the processes of maturation and development discussed here. This is not so. Creativity depends for its existence and direction upon the individual's existing orientation to relevant information and willingness to make the efforts necessary in locating it. As Case (1978, p. 65) noted, what any child can learn from any "given experience is a function of his general developmental level."

Over the years, a number of research reports have appeared that bear directly on this development. Three that are most relevant here are those of Getzels and Jackson (1962), Crandall and Battle (1970), and MacKinnon (1982). Although their subjects were gifted adolescents, average adolescents in terms of their IQs, and gifted adult males, respectively, they agree in giving substantial evidence of how widely their subjects can differ in terms of being creative, interested more in intellectual activities than routine academic achievement, and creative and productive in their careers. Just as interesting and important, the pictures of the types of families involved in these developmental outcomes are basically the same for all three projects, despite the differences among the subject populations. To be brief, the families least likely to have members (adult or young) who are identifiably creative are the ones that put a premium on maintaining emotional stability and displaying what is for them acceptable good behavior. These families show a clear understanding and sense of boundaries in relationships, of the importance of efforts for achievement in conventional subjects and careers, and of the accepted method of achievement. The families who are the mirror images (opposites) of the more convention-bound families are the ones from which the great majority of creative children, adolescents, adults, and eminent men and women come. There is another difference between the two groups of families, as well as among their members. Those families that have more creativity are usually more complex, varied, and expressive than the others. (This body of research is examined in more detail elsewhere; see Albert, 1994b, 1994c, in press.)

Educational Impediments

The same conditions that influence how children learn to cope with novelty, gaps, and separation also influence not only their creativity but the direction and range of their education, especially in the blanket importance that education gives to clarity and conventionality in schoolwork.

Many researchers (summarized by Wakefield, in press) have identified what can be called a dead period between the ages of nine and twelve in which signs of early creativity drop out of sight; a time when conventional behavior is most stressed. (Something similar to this was reported by Getzels and Jackson (1962) among very gifted adolescents.) It is clear that this emphasis can have a significant effect on how adolescents approach their schoolwork in general as well as their more specific preferences for either academics or intellectual activities. Often families and schools share a common emphasis on precise and clear thinking and on well-organized learning skills (which implies they are also well controlled). They emphasize working on well-defined problems with clean results and getting good grades that can be compared to others. With this dynamic in action, it is no wonder that little creativity is seen in schools or during adolescence, even if the potential for it survived through childhood. Wakefield observed, "This period of acceleration in skill acquisition is accompanied by declines in creative thinking."

What Wakefield observed for adolescents is to some extent the precursor of what Cutrona and others (1994) reported—that college students' perception of parents' and friends' emotional support and encouragement can often favorably influence their academic achievement, but not their creative efforts. These educational results are more than the consequences of educational practices, but they are also defensive, and therefore, in close agreement with Swanson's (1988) conclusion that one of the purposes of all defense mechanisms is to legitimize the individual's behavior both internally and to significant others. This holds especially true in adolescence.

The research cited here seriously questions whether children in general are as creative as many of us would like to believe. Just as important, it raises the question of whether preadolescent children or adolescents can be deliberately taught to be creative. If one takes seriously a review by Feldhusen (1991) of research on the effects of formal instruction in creativity for gifted children, we have little grounds for optimism—the results reported by Feldhusen are limited in their scope and duration. Although a number of children come away from such instruction with more positive feelings about themselves (especially in leadership roles), their training in creativity fails to transfer beyond academics into areas that differ from those in which instruction was originally given, in agreement with Siegler and Kotovsky's (1993) analysis of why the types of creativity seen in schools and the real world are so different, and Brody and Stanley's (1991) research reporting that the benefits to older gifted students of their accelerated and special educational training are limited to their academic successes, but not to their creativity.

Conclusion

Although I do not like ending on a pessimistic note, I believe that the facts tell us that we generally overestimate the ease and naturalness of the development of creativity in childhood, and even more so, past it. One of the reasons for this is that we also underestimate the power of family and societal injunctions to be, above all, effective and recognizably conventional in and outside school. Especially underestimated is how early in children's development all this starts and creativity's difficulties begin. The reader may have noticed that I have said little about giftedness and talent. This was not an oversight. Even when they are clearly present, their full development is contingent upon the more basic conditions and experiences the chapter explores. On the basis of my own and many others' research, I am certain of this, just as I am certain that the development of a child's giftedness or talent will more often reflect the child's family than change it.

References

Ainsworth, M.D.S. "The Development of Infant-Mother Attachment." In B. M. Caldwell and H. N. Ricciuti (eds.), *Review of Child Development Research,* Vol. 3. Chicago: University of Chicago Press, 1973.

Albert, R. S. "Cognitive Development and Parental Loss Among the Gifted, the Exceptionally Gifted and the Creative." *Psychological Reports,* 1971, *29,* 19–26.

Albert, R. S. "Toward Behavioral Definition of Genius." *American Psychologist,* 1975, *30,* 140–151.

Albert, R. S. "Family Position and the Attainment of Eminence." *Gifted Child Quarterly,* 1980, *24,* 87–89.

Albert, R. S. "The Achievement of Eminence: A Longitudinal Study of Exceptionally Gifted Boys and Their Families." In R. F. Subotnik and K. D. Arnold (eds.), *Beyond Terman: Contemporary Longitudinal Studies of Giftedness and Talent.* Norwood, N.J.: Ablex, 1994a.

Albert, R. S. "The Contribution of Early Family History to the Achievement of Eminence." In N. Colangelo and S. Assouline (eds.), *Wallace National Research Symposium on Talent Development.* Columbus: Ohio Psychology, 1994b.

Albert, R. S. "What the Study of Eminence Can Teach Us." Paper presented at the American Psychological Association 102nd annual convention, Los Angeles, Aug. 12–16, 1994c. (APA Tape 94–278.)

Albert, R. S. "The Achievement of Eminence as an Evolutionary Strategy." In M. A. Runco (ed.), *Creativity Research Handbook,* Vol. 2. Cresskill, N.J.: Hampton Press, in press.

Albert, R. S., and Runco, M. A. "Possible Different Personality Dispositions of Scientists and Non-Scientists." In D. Jackson and J. P. Rushton (eds.) *Scientific Excellence: Origins and Assessments.* Thousand Oaks, Calif.: Sage, 1987.

Albert, R. S., and Runco, M. A. "Independence and Cognitive Ability in Gifted and Exceptionally Gifted Boys." *Journal of Youth and Adolescence,* 1989, *18,* 221–230.

Amato, P. R., and Keith B. "Parental Divorce and the Well-Being of Children: A Meta-Analysis." *Psychological Bulletin,* 1991, *110,* 26–43.

Baillargeon, R., and DeVos, J. "Object Permanence in Young Infants: Further Evidence." *Child Development,* 1991, *62,* 1227–1246.

Barron, F. "Complexity-Simplicity as a Personality Dimension." *Journal of Abnormal-Social Psychology,* 1953, *48,* 163–172.

Berrington, H. "Prime Ministers and the Search for Love." In R. S. Albert (ed.), *Genius and Eminence: The Social Psychology of Creativity and Exceptional Achievement.* New York: Pergamon Press, 1983.

Bond, M., Gardiner, S. T., and Sigal, J. "An Empirical Examination of Defense Mechanisms." *Archives of General Psychiatry,* 1983, *40,* 333–338.

Bowlby, J. *Attachment and Loss,* Vol. 2: *Separation: Anxiety and Anger.* New York: Basic Books, 1973.

Brody, L. E., and Stanley, J. C. "Young College Students: Assessing Factors That Contribute to Success." In W. T. Southern and E. D. Jones (eds.), *The Academic Acceleration of Gifted Children.* New York: Teachers College Press, 1991.

Brody, L. R., Rozek, M. K., and Muten, E. O. "Age, Sex and Individual Differences in Children's Defensive Styles." *Journal of Clinical Child Psychology,* 1985, *14,* 132–138.

Case, R. "Intellectual Development from Birth to Adulthood: A Neo-Piagetian Interpretation." In R. S. Siegler (ed.), *Children's Thinking: What Develops.* Hillsdale, N.J.: Erlbaum, 1978.

Cleiver, M.P.H. *Bereavement and Adaptation: A Comparative Study of the Aftermath of Death.* Washington, D.C.: Hemisphere, 1993.

Cramer, P. *The Development of Defense Mechanisms: Theory, Research and Assessment.* New York: Springer-Verlag, 1991.

Crandall, V. C., and Battle, E. S. "The Antecedents and Adult Correlates of Academic and Intellectual Achievement Effort." In J. P. Hill (ed.), *Minnesota Symposium on Child Development,* Vol. 4. St. Paul: University of Minnesota Press, 1970.

Cutrona, C. E., and others. "Perceived Parental Social Support and Academic Achievement: An Attachment Theory Perspective." *Journal of Personality and Social Psychology,* 1994, *66* (2), 369–378.

Edel, L. "The Madness of Art." *American Journal of Psychiatry,* 1975, *132,* 1005–1012.

Erikson, E. H. *Identity and the Life Cycle: Selected Papers, Psychological Issues.* Monograph No. 1, Vol. 1. Madison, Conn.: International University Press, 1959.

Feldhusen, J. I. "Effects of Programs for the Gifted: A Search for Evidence." In W. T. Southern and E. D. Jones (eds.), *The Academic Acceleration of Gifted Children.* New York: Teachers College Press, 1991.

Fergusson, D. M., Lynskey, M. T., and Horwood, J. J. "The Effects of Parental Separation, the Timing of Separation and Gender on Children's Performance on Cognitive Tests." *Journal of Children's Psychology and Psychiatry,* 1994, *35,* 1077–1099.

Freud, A. *The Ego and the Mechanisms of Defense.* Madison, Conn.: International University Press, 1936.

Freud, S. "The Interpretation of Dreams." In J. Strachey (ed. and trans.), *The Standard Edition of the Complete Psychological Works of Sigmund Freud.* Vols. 4 and 5. London: Hogarth Press, 1953. (Originally published 1900.)

Freud, S. "The Neuro-Psychoses of Defense." *Standard Edition,* 3, 45–61. London: Hogarth Press, 1966. (Originally published 1894.)

Getzels, J. W., and Jackson, P. W. *Creativity and Intelligence: Explorations with Gifted Students.* New York: Wiley, 1962.

Goertzel, V., and Goertzel, M. G. *Cradles of Eminence.* London: Constable, 1962.

Haan, N. "Proposed Model of Ego Functioning: Coping and Defense Mechanisms in Relationship to I.Q. Change." *Psychological Monographs,* 1963, *77,* 1–23.

Haan, N. *Coping and Defending: Processes of Self-Environmental Organizations.* New York: Academic Press, 1977.

Hedges, L. V., and Nowell, A. "Sex Differences in Mental Test Scores, Variability and Numbers of High-Scoring Individuals." *Science,* 1995, *269,* 41–45.

Helson, R. "Writers and Artists: Two Types of Vocational Consciousness in the Art System." *Journal of Vocational Behavior,* 1978, *12,* 351–363.

Helson, R. "Which of Those Young Women with Creative Potential Became Productive? Personality in College and Characteristics of Parents." In R. Hogan (ed.), *Perspectives in Personality,* Vol. 1. Greenwich, Conn.: JAI Press, 1985.

Hull, D. L. *Science as a Process: An Evolutionary Account of the Social and Conceptual Development of Science.* Chicago: University of Chicago Press, 1988.

Jacobson, A. M., and others. "An Approach to Evaluating Adolescent Ego Defense Mechanisms Using Clinical Interviews." In G. E. Vaillant (ed.), *Empirical Studies of Ego Mechanisms of Defense.* Washington, D.C.: American Psychiatric Press, 1986.

Kagan, J. "A Conception of Early Adolescence." *Daedalus,* 1971, *100,* 997–1012.

Keller, H., and Boigs, R. "The Development of Exploratory Behavior." In M. E. Lamb and H. Keller (eds.), *Infant Development: Perspectives from German-Speaking Countries.* Hillsdale, N.J.: Erlbaum, 1991.

Kubie, L. *The Neurotic Distortion of the Creative Process.* Lawrence: University of Kansas Press, 1958.

Levit, D. B. "The Development of Ego Defenses in Adolescence. *Journal of Youth and Adolescence,* 1993, *22,* 493–512.

Loevinger, J., and Wessler, R. *Measuring Ego Development, I. Construction and Use of a Sentence Completion Test.* San Francisco: Jossey-Bass, 1970.

Loewenstein, G. "The Psychology of Curiosity: A Review and Re-Interpretation." *Psychological Bulletin,* 1994, *116,* 75–98.

Ludwig, A. M. *The Price of Greatness: Resolving the Creativity and Madness Controversy.* New York: Guilford Press, 1994.

Lund, D. A., Caserta, M. S., and Dimond, M. A. "The Course of Spousal Bereavement in

Later Life." In M. S. Stroebe, W. Stroebe, and R. O. Hansson (eds.), *Handbook of Bereavement: Theory, Research and Intervention.* New York: Cambridge University Press, 1993.

MacKinnon, D. W. *In Search of Human Effectiveness: Identifying and Developing Creativity.* Buffalo, N.Y.: Creative Education Foundation, 1978.

MacKinnon, D. W. "The Highly Effective Individual." In R. S. Albert (ed.), *Genius and Eminence.* (2nd ed.) New York: Pergamon Press, 1993.

Martindale, C. "Father's Absence, Psycho-Pathology, and Poetic Eminence." *Psychological Reports,* 1972, *31,* 843–847.

Miller, D. R., and Swanson, G. E. *Inner Conflict and Defense.* Austin, Tex.: Holt, Rinehart and Winston, 1960.

Piaget, J. *The Origins of Intelligence in Children.* Madison, Conn.: International Universities Press, 1952.

Raskin, E. A. "Comparison of Scientific and Literary Ability: A Biological Study of Eminent Scientists and Men of Letters of the Nineteenth Century." *Journal of Abnormal and Social Psychology,* 1936, *31,* 20–35.

Raz-Kohen, R. *Psychobiological Aspects of Cognitive Growth.* New York: Academic Press, 1977.

Sanders, C. M. "Risk Factors in Bereavement Outcome." In M. S. Stroebe, W. Stroebe, and R. D. Hansson (eds.), *Handbook of Bereavement: Theory, Research and Intervention.* New York: Cambridge University Press, 1993.

Shepard, D. M., and Barrclough, B. M. "The Aftermath of Parental Suicide for Children." *British Journal of Psychiatry,* 1976, *129,* 267–276.

Siegler, R. S. *Children's Thinking.* Englewood Cliffs, N.J.: Prentice Hall, 1986.

Siegler, R. S., and Kotovsky, K. "Two Levels of Giftedness: Shall Ever the Twain Meet?" In R. S. Albert (ed.), *Genius and Eminence.* (2nd ed.) Oxford: Pergamon Press, 1993.

Silverman, P. R., and Worden, J. W. "Children's Reactions to the Death of a Parent." In M. S. Stroebe, W. Stroebe, and R. O. Hansson (eds.), *Handbook of Bereavement: Theory, Research and Intervention.* New York: Cambridge University Press, 1993.

Smith, G.J.W., and Carlsson, I. "Creativity in Early and Middle School Years." *International Journal of Behavioral Development,* 1983, *6,* 167–195.

Smith, G.J.W., and Carlsson, I. M. *The Creative Process: A Functional Model Based on Empirical Studies From Early Childhood to Middle Age.* Madison, Conn.: International Universities Press, 1990.

Smith, G.J.W., and Danielson, A. *Anxiety and Defensive Strategies in Childhood and Adolescence.* Madison, Conn.: International Universities Press, 1982.

Stern, D. N. *The Interpersonal World of the Infant.* New York: Basic Books, 1985.

Swanson, G. E. "Determinants of the Individual's Defenses Against Inner Conflicts: Review and Reformulation." In J. C. Glidewell (ed.), *Parental Attitudes and Child Behavior.* Springfield, Ill.: Thomas, 1961.

Swanson, G. E. *Ego Defenses and the Legitimation of Behavior.* New York: Cambridge University Press, 1988.

Vaillant, G. E. *Adaptation to Life.* Boston: Little, Brown, 1977.

Vaillant, G. E., Bond, M., and Vaillant, C. O. "An Empirically Validated Hierarchy of Defense Mechanisms." *Archives of General Psychiatry,* 1985, *43,* 786–794.

Wakefield, J. In M. A. Runco (ed.), *Critical Creative Processes.* Cresskill, N.J.: Hampton Press, in press.

Waterman, C. K., and Waterman, A. S. "Ego Identity Status and Decision Styles." *Journal of Youth and Adolescence,* 1974, *3,* 1–6.

Weinstock, A. R. "Family Environment and the Development of Defense and Coping Mechanisms." *Journal of Personality and Social Psychology,* 1967, *5,* 67–75.

Winnicott, D. W. "Playing: Creative Activity and the Search for the Self." In D. W. Winnicott, *Playing and Reality.* New York: Basic Books, 1971.

Winnicott, D. W. *The Maturational Processes and the Facilitating Environment: Studies in the Theory of Emotional Development.* London: Hogarth Press, 1976.

ROBERT S. ALBERT is professor emeritus of psychology at Pitzer College, Claremont, California.

An idea used by Darwin to explain the great difference in mental powers between the higher animals and humans while arguing for our continuity with them is used as the source analogy to explain the relationship between creativity in childhood and creativity in adulthood.

Creativity from Childhood to Adulthood: A Difference of Degree and Not of Kind

Robert T. Keegan

In 1871, Charles Darwin's *The Descent of Man* was published. In that book, for the first time, Darwin explicitly made the case that humans were descended in a series of small modifications from some ape-like ancestor, that our species had evolved as all others had through natural selection, and, as a result, genuine continuity existed between humans and the other animals populating the earth. He marshaled the evidence for evolutionary continuity by citing anatomical and physiological similarities between our species and the great apes, crafting an argument that many eventually accepted as a compelling case for the natural evolution of the human body. But when it came to explaining the qualities of mind possessed by our species, our mental and moral capacities, many, including the coframer of the principle of natural selection, Alfred Russel Wallace, saw the divide between humans and even the intelligent creatures most anatomically and physiologically similar, such as the chimpanzee, to be so wide as to shatter the idea of an all embracing continuity between humans and the rest of the animal kingdom. Humans seemed anomalous. Wallace and others invoked a supernatural agency to explain the origin of our mental and moral capacities, seeing these capacities as fundamentally different in kind from those possessed by all other creatures. Darwin's tricky problem in *Descent of Man* was to account for the admittedly great divide between the mental and moral capacities of humans and all other creatures while simultaneously making the case for our common descent and essential continuity with them. After plainly admitting, "There can be no doubt that the difference between the mind of the lowest man and that of the highest animal is immense" ([1871] 1981, p. 104),

Darwin wrote in the next paragraph, "Nevertheless the difference in mind between man and the higher animals, great as it is, is certainly one of degree and not of kind" ([1871] 1981, p. 105).

The Source Analogy

Why raise the issue of evolution in a forum devoted to exploring the development of creativity throughout the life span? I want to be clear at the outset that I am not attempting to revive Haeckel's notion that "ontogeny recapitulates phylogeny," that the development of an individual child repeats in compressed time the evolution of our species. I am not suggesting that children are little animals who reach human status only in adulthood. I am suggesting that the task Darwin faced in *Descent of Man,* accounting for the mental and moral uniqueness of our species while simultaneously arguing for our essential continuity with other species, is analogous to the issue under consideration here, exploring the nature of the connection between creativity in childhood and creativity in adulthood, especially creative thinking at its Olympian heights in adulthood represented by innovators such as Newton, Darwin, van Gogh, and Einstein. The creativity of individuals such as these may seem as far removed— as anomalous—from the creativity found in a child as the mental capacity of humans seems removed from the intellect of the chimpanzee, but the study of creative adults and studies of the cognitive abilities of children show their essential continuity. Holyoak and Thagard (1995) have described how one idea can be used as a source analogy for understanding and explaining a new or target area, as long as "natural correspondences" exist between the source and the target (p. 200). I perceive natural correspondences between the task Darwin confronted in *Descent* to explain interspecies differences in mental functioning and our efforts to understand human creativity across the life span. Darwin's strategy for explaining our species' close continuity with the higher animals while simultaneously accounting for our uniqueness can therefore serve as the source analogy for the target under consideration here, how to understand the relationship between creative thinking in childhood and creative thinking in adulthood as its highest level.

On Continuity

First, to the issue of continuity in this analogy. Darwin applied two strategies for bridging the gap between the mentality of animals and humans: he demystified the mental powers of humans, showing they are built upon the mental capacities possessed by animals and are not unique to our species. He then raised the mental powers of animals, showing them to be more humanlike than previously considered.

We can apply the same strategies to explain differences in creative thinking across the life span, demystify the thinking of outstanding creative thinkers, and raise the status of the child's cognitive abilities.

I am one of a group of researchers using the cognitive case study to investigate creative thinking in adulthood. In this approach, the investigator carries out an intensive study of the development of one person's thinking as that individual thinker constructs the creative accomplishment for which he or she becomes known. The particular model of case study investigation we use was developed by Gruber (1989) and is called the "evolving systems approach." In this approach, three aspects of the individual are probed with special attention: the individual's organization of knowledge, organization of purpose, and organization of affect. I will illustrate these concepts by relating them to a clear case of high-level creativity in adulthood—Charles Darwin.

How Darwin acquired his knowledge is a fascinating story of an individual's movement from amateur to journeyman to expert in his chosen domain, but a detailed account of this progression would require many more pages than are available here. However, it is possible to economically convey an impression of how Darwin organized his knowledge. Darwin and other creative thinkers use an "ensemble of metaphors" (Osowski, 1989) and "images of wide scope" (Gruber, 1978) to compress and emphasize different aspects of the issues about which they think. Several images were particularly important for Darwin in organizing his thinking about nature and in expressing his views to an audience he knew would be skeptical (see Gruber, 1978). The *tree of life* image, which appeared in Darwin's first notebook on transmutation (Barrett and others, 1987, pp. 177, 180) and again in *Origin of Species* ([1859] 1964, p. 116), highlights the common descent of all nature from a single trunk while emphasizing its branching diversity. The image of "a force like a hundred thousand wedges trying [to] force every kind of adapted structure into the gaps in the œconomy of Nature, or rather forming gaps by thrusting out weaker ones" (Barrett and others, 1987, p. 375) focuses attention on the intense struggle for existence in nature and the resultant extinction of those who get pushed out of the economy of nature. The tree of life and wedges images appear early in Darwin's thinking and persist through the first edition of *Origin,* a period of over twenty years. The third image also had a long gestation, but its final form differs from its precursors in the notebooks. However, its importance to Darwin is evident from its strategic placement in *Origin,* beginning the final paragraph of the book: "It is interesting to contemplate an entangled bank, clothed with many plants of many kinds, with birds singing on the bushes, with various insects flitting about, and with worms crawling through the damp earth, and to reflect that these elaborately constructed forms, so different from each other, and dependent on each other in so complex a manner, have all been produced by laws acting around us" (p. 489). This image emphasizes the fullness of nature and the interdependency of its various life forms—an ecological perspective.

It was through images such as these that Darwin organized his vast knowledge of natural history. The ability to use images of this sort is not unique to Darwin. It does not signify a special genius way of thinking that is outside the reach of more ordinary thinkers. In fact, throughout his notebooks, there is no evidence of any special genius thought process unique to Darwin. There is, however, ample evidence for Darwin's capacity to work hard in acquiring an extraordinary body of knowledge in the various departments of natural history.

Purposes, the factors that motivate an individual, are gauged by what the person did, the activities or enterprises he or she pursued (Gruber, 1989, pp. 11–14). Mapping and compressing what the individual did can be achieved through the construction of a chart, diagram, graph, or some other pictorial representation. Constructing a network of enterprise for Darwin shows how he was motivated to pursue the study of geology, zoology, psychology, and botany at different times throughout his life (Gruber and Davis, 1988, p. 254). One hint at the depth of his motivation and commitment to understand nature is the eight consecutive years he spent working out the classification of barnacles.

The creative individual has an important emotional relationship with his or her work. Again using Darwin to illustrate the point, an early childhood habit of taking long, solitary walks and collecting all manner of natural objects, horseback riding through the Welsh hills in early adolescence, a passion for hunting birds and the serious collection and study of marine invertebrates during mid-adolescence, a zeal for collecting and classifying beetles in late adolescence, a voyage around the world as ship's naturalist as a young adult, followed by a lifetime of the study of nature—all attest to Darwin's intense love of the natural world. This love of nature was wedded to a growing love of science in mid- to late adolescence, a period of life that should receive greater attention in the study of creativity. At least in the cases of two highly creative thinkers, Darwin and Einstein, finding a supportive environment in mid-adolescence where they could pursue their interests in a way that felt natural and comfortable—Darwin at Edinburgh and Einstein in Aarau—enabled them to get started on the work that resulted in their creative achievements (Keegan, in press).

Summing up then, the highly creative adult shows a deep knowledge of his or her subject matter, is intrinsically motivated to work hard in the area, and has a strong emotional bond with what he or she is doing. In the case of Darwin, and in case studies of other highly creative adults, there is no evidence for any unique thought process, or for that matter any unique motivational or emotional component, that cannot be found in more ordinary individuals. The components are highly refined and highly organized, like the excellent performance of a finely tuned engine, but no special single component makes the difference. The work of Gruber and his colleagues using the evolving systems approach (Wallace and Gruber, 1989) and the work of others such as Gardner (1994) and Weisberg (1993) have helped to demystify the thought processes of highly creative individuals. In fact, case studies of Darwin (Gruber, 1974; Keegan, 1989), Wordsworth (Jeffrey, 1989), van Gogh (Brower, in press), and Dali (Schwartz, 1993) have shown the great amount of repetition that occurs in the work of creative people. Repetition has not usually been conceived of as the hallmark of innovative thinking, but case studies of creative individuals at work reveal how novelty emerges from the process of reworking with slight variation an idea, image, or technique. These studies also demonstrate that there are different pathways to creative achievement.

Creativity in Childhood

Having characterized creative production in adults as the result of acquiring and organizing knowledge, being motivated to work hard in an area, and loving the work, the question is whether or not some children are capable of the same?

The answer, I believe, is yes.

First, consider a child's organization of knowledge. Anyone who has had regular contact with children over the past few years has probably come across a child, or more than one, who has a prodigious knowledge of dinosaurs. It is not that such children can just name and identify a lot of dinosaurs and tell you whether they were meat eaters or plant eaters—they can tell you whether the creatures lived in the Triassic, Jurassic, or Cretaceous period and that the impact crater from the asteroid that led to their extinction sixty-four million years ago can be found in the Yucatan Peninsula of Mexico. Children are certainly capable of amassing and organizing a significant body of knowledge. They are capable of using analogy, imagery, metaphor, and other thought processes involved in creative thinking.

Do children have purposes? Do they have the motivation to work hard to achieve some end? Do they have *enterprises*—activities that they engage in over extended periods of time? Again, the answer is yes. Some children keep at an activity or a subject area for years, whether it be dinosaurs, drawing, collecting, or roller blading. As with creative adults, some of the motivation sustaining the activity may be extrinsic—wanting to be smarter than a friend about dinosaurs or to win in a race, but intrinsic motivation is also in evidence when a child intensely pursues an activity alone and on her own, acquires a new item for a collection that involves no competition with a friend, or draws the same object over and over again just to get it right.

Finally, can some children develop a passion for a certain subject matter or activity? Once again, the answer is yes. *Bookworm* and *gym rat* are terms describing the child who falls in love with reading or basketball. When parents place time limits on Nintendo play, they illustrate one response to an activity the child falls in love with but the parents consider to be unproductive. Interestingly, Darwin may have disagreed with such restrictions. In a letter to American educator Emily Talbot concerning whether parents should try to direct the child toward productive and constructive activities, Darwin wrote, "It may be more beneficial that a child should follow energetically some pursuit, of however trifling a nature, and thus acquire perseverance, than that he should be turned from it, because of no future advantage to him" (Barrett, 1977, pp. 232–233).

Perseverance is a product of loving an activity and being motivated to pursue it. It results in the accumulation of more and more knowledge or skill in the chosen area. Perseverance has been well documented in the case of creative adults. Gardner (1994) recently agreed with an earlier suggestion by Hayes (1981) that it takes an individual approximately ten years to have a first creative breakthrough. This time frame seems just about right. Even prodigies work hard. It took Mozart ten years before he produced a composition of the quality for which his music is now remembered (Weisberg, 1993). It is a shame that the empirical base for studying individual children over extended periods of time, years for example, is relatively weak, except, possibly, for the study of language development. There was a tradition of keeping careful records of the development of individual children, of keeping baby or child diaries, and some of the founders of the field of developmental psychology such as Darwin, Preyer, Baldwin, and Piaget kept diaries of their children. The observations they recorded were very influential in forming their ideas, but this tradition faded from American psychology in the early decades of this century as survey and experimental methods came to dominate (Wallace, Franklin, and Keegan, 1994). There are, however, retrospective studies of the childhood production of individuals who gain prominence in adulthood, such as Pariser's (1991) study of the juvenile artistic development of Klee, Lautrec, and Picasso, which attests to these individuals' persistence. So as Darwin demystified the mental capacities of humans to show them to be of the same kind as those of animals, case study research has helped to demystify the processes involved in creative thinking, showing them to be of the same kind used by others, and of which children, at least older children, are capable.

With respect to raising the status of the child's mental capacities in line with Darwin's strategy of raising the status of animals' mental capacities, throughout this century research on the cognitive development of children has revealed greater and greater competencies at earlier and earlier ages. Piaget has been a dominant voice in this regard. As Piaget and others have raised the mental status of children by showing the interior logic and system to their way of thinking, they have succeeded in shrinking the gap between the mind of the child and the mind of the adult.

On Differences

Having presented the case for basic continuity in the processes involved in creativity in childhood and adulthood, how do I account for the great difference of degree between the creative child and a Darwin, Einstein, or Picasso? Returning to our source analogy, how did Darwin account for the great difference in degree between the mentality of the higher animals and the mentality of humans? Reminding his readers that animals had the ability to communicate through vocalizations, so humans were not unique in this regard, nevertheless Darwin outlined a scenario in which the evolution of articulate language brought our species over what I would characterize as a *cognitive threshold*. A threshold, a point of change, can be crossed in a number of different ways. One way is through the continuation of an ordinary process that previously produced no dramatic change. The camel suffers no permanent disability as straw upon straw is added to its back until the addition of just one more straw exceeds the load-bearing capacity of its backbone. As Darwin wrote in *Descent*, "If it be maintained that certain powers, such as self-consciousness, abstraction, &c., are peculiar to man, it may well be that these are the incidental results of other highly-advanced intellectual faculties; and these again are mainly the result of the continued use of a highly developed language" (p. 105).

The evolution of language was the final straw. It is interesting to note that a number of archeologists and paleoanthropologists have suggested that a threshold was crossed in human evolution between forty-five thousand and thirty thousand years ago, at the start of the Upper Paleolithic, resulting in an explosion of creative activities that produced what we call *culture,* and they concur with Darwin that this threshold was crossed because of the evolution of symbolic behavior, the use of spoken language and pictures to communicate meaning (Kuper, 1994, pp. 82–83). The most recent cave paintings found in the Ardèche region of southern France have been dated to over thirty thousand years ago, and individual differences in artistic skill have been detected. Not everyone became a skilled artist even then. Symbolic behavior provided a platform for creative production; it did not ensure it. It was a necessary but not a sufficient condition.

What then is the parallel in individual adult creativity? What is the component in the development of the thinking of an adult that carries that person over the threshold from competent but ordinary thinker to extraordinary and creative thinker, a step which is analogous to the evolution of language in our species that enabled us to cross over a threshold and become what I would call *Homo cultus* (cultured man), an innovation that produced a great difference between our species and all others? My candidate is the acquisition of *expert knowledge*. Acquiring expert knowledge is a necessary though not a sufficient condition to foster creativity at the highest levels, just as the development of symbolic activity in our species did not result in everyone becoming an extraordinary artist. Building expert knowledge takes a long time. The child, and likely the adolescent, has not had enough time to acquire expert knowledge, that is, to absorb the canon, to form an image of wide scope, to organize his or her knowledge to the extent that an adult has. This is not to suggest that there are no differences in purpose or affect between the creative child and the creative adult. There is a predictable cognitive dissonance effect of effort justification. The longer the activity has continued, the more the individual will have a need to justify the work and effort put into it, making it harder to walk away from the activity the longer one has pursued it. Long work on a problem may also bring with it the sense of ownership of that problem, which would help sustain the work. For example, in Darwin's notebooks on human evolution, there is a significant shift from the use of phrases such as "my father says" and "my father thinks," to "my view," "my idea," and "my theory" (Keegan and Gruber, 1994). Affective changes are also likely to occur as the duration of an enterprise increases. So the whole system of the creative adult may be developed to a greater degree than in the child. However, it is the acquisition of expert knowledge, in my view, that is the primary vehicle for carrying the adult over the threshold into the highest levels of creative production, differentiating that adult not only from children but from other adults as well. Expert knowledge in geology formed Darwin's source analogy for understanding new and unfamiliar material. He took a basic theme from uniformitarian geology that change occurs gradually over long periods of time (noting, for example, that the Andes were raised inch by inch over the eons) and then applied this basic theme of gradualism to explain phenomena as diverse as coral reef formation, the creation of topsoil, and the origin of species (Keegan, 1989).

The point, at first, may seem oxymoronic—a genuine contradiction in terms, but upon reflection is merely paradoxical—only seemingly contradictory: a person must first become a traditionalist in the field before becoming an innovator in it. Most children will not master their chosen fields, but for the adult who does, the acquisition of expert knowledge grounds that individual in the tradition of the field, and this grounding is necessary for informed and productive departure from that tradition. Darwin absorbed traditional views on natural history through teachers such as Henslow and Lyell before he offered a radical transformation of the field (Gruber, 1974). Picasso worked through traditional techniques of art, guided in childhood by his father, before he developed Cubism (Gardner, 1994, pp. 137–185). Stravinsky mastered traditional Russian musical styles and techniques under the tutelage of Nikolay Rimsky-Korsakov before he shocked the musical world with his radical departures from the musical conventions of the times (Gardner, 1994, pp. 187–226). Dick Fosbury, gold medalist in the high jump at the 1968 Mexico City Olympic games, worked hard during several periods of his training in high jumping to master the traditional straddle-style jump before he revolutionized high jumping with his radical, 90° to the bar approach—his back-to-the-bar, missile-like self-projection of the "Fosbury flop" (Blount, 1969). Acquiring expert knowledge of the traditional views in a field may be a prerequisite for discerning its limitations, and discerning its limitations may be the spur to constructing a new point of view to explain the known facts of the field, for uncovering new facts, or for developing new techniques to overcome the limitations of the old.

Gruber (1974) has characterized the great accomplishment of the creative thinker as the construction of a new point of view. Creative thinkers develop a unique way of organizing the materials of their chosen domain. Darwin provided a new way of viewing the facts of biogeography, biological diversity, embryology, and taxonomy. Einstein's unique point of view was that it was necessary to consider an observer's point of view in explaining phenomena in physics. Joyce provided a reader with a new point of view by portraying the uncensored interior stream of consciousness of a character—a unique portrayal of a character's point of view. Van Gogh constructed a point of view in which he strove to express his strong emotional relationship with nature rather than a veridical portrayal of it, a strategy that resulted in the thrusting perspective, bold colors, thick brush strokes, and swirls characteristic of his mature signature style. It takes a long time to construct a unique point of view, to absorb the canon, to perceive its limitations and then go beyond it, and this process will usually bring a person into the early adult phase of life.

Conclusions

The cognitive case study of individual creative adults has contributed valuable ideas to our collective effort to understand creativity. The close study of individual children and adolescents over extended periods of time would further illuminate the development of creative thinking across the life span and help us understand the continuum of creative thinking from a child to a Newton. Here the task is easier than the one Darwin set for himself in *Descent of Man:* "In a future chapter I shall make some few remarks on the probable steps and means by which the several mental and moral faculties of man have been gradually evolved. That this at least is possible ought not to be denied, when we daily see their development in every infant; and when we may trace a perfect gradation from the mind of an utter idiot, lower than that of the lowest animal, to the mind of a Newton" (p. 106).

The gap between the bright creative child and the creative adult is not nearly so wide as the gap Darwin sought to bridge in *Descent.* There is substantial continuity between the creative child and the creative adult because both use ordinary thought processes in the construction of their novel and valued creations. The accumulation of knowledge, the sense of purpose, and the love of work exhibited by adults who produce something of extraordinary novelty and value are approximated by children and adolescents in their pursuits and underpin their creative productions. As the evolution of language carried our species over a cognitive threshhold permitting a burst of creativity, acquiring expert knowledge can carry the individual to a previously unattainable level of creative thinking. Great as it may seem, and great as it may be, the difference between the processes of thought, motivations, and emotions of the creative child and the processes of thought, motivations, and emotions of a Darwin or Newton is, nevertheless, "certainly one of degree and not of kind."

References

Barrett, P. H. (ed.). *The Collected Papers of Charles Darwin.* Chicago: University of Chicago Press, 1977.

Barrett, P. H., and others, (eds.). *Charles Darwin's Notebooks, 1836–1844: Geology, Transmutation of Species, Metaphysical Enquiries.* Ithaca, N.Y.: Cornell University Press, 1987.

Blount, R., Jr., "Being Backward Gets Results." *Sports Illustrated,* 1969, *30* (6), 24–27.

Brower, R. "Getting Started: Vincent van Gogh's First Two Years as an Artist." *Journal of Adult Development,* in press.

Darwin, C. *On the Origin of Species by Means of Natural Selection, or the Preservation of Favoured Races in the Struggle for Life.* Cambridge, Mass.: Harvard University Press, 1964. (Originally published 1859.)

Darwin, C. *The Descent of Man and Selection in Relation to Sex.* Princeton, N.J.,: Princeton University Press, 1981. (Originally published 1871.)

Gardner, H. *Creating Minds: An Anatomy of Creativity Seen Through the Lives of Freud, Einstein, Picasso, Stravinsky, Eliot, Graham, and Gandhi.* New York: Basic Books, 1994.

Gruber, H. E. *Darwin on Man: A Psychological Study of Creativity, Together with Darwin's Early and Unpublished Notebooks,* transcribed and annotated by Paul H. Barrett. New York: Dutton, 1974.

Gruber, H. E. "Darwin's 'Tree of Nature' and Other Images of Wide Scope." In J. Wechsler (ed.), *On Aesthetics in Science.* Cambridge, Mass.: MIT Press, 1978.

Gruber, H. E. "The Evolving Systems Approach to Creative Work." In D. B. Wallace and H. E. Gruber (eds.), *Creative People at Work: Twelve Cognitive Case Studies.* New York: Oxford University Press, 1989.

Gruber, H. E., and Davis, S. N. "Inching Our Way Up Mount Olympus: The Evolving Systems Approach to Creative Thinking." In R. J. Sternberg (ed.), *The Nature of Creativity: Contemporary Psychological Perspectives.* New York: Cambridge University Press, 1988.

Hayes, J. R. *The Complete Problem Solver.* Philadephia: Franklin Institute Press, 1981.

Holyoak, K. J., and Thagard, P. *Mental Leaps: Analogy in Creative Thought.* Cambridge, Mass.: MIT Press, 1995.

Jeffrey, L. R. "Writing and Rewriting Poetry: William Wordsworth." In D. B. Wallace and H. E. Gruber (eds.), *Creative People at Work: Twelve Cognitive Case Studies.* New York: Oxford University Press, 1989.

Keegan, R. T. "How Charles Darwin Became a Psychologist." In D. B. Wallace and H. E. Gruber (eds.), *Creative People at Work: Twelve Cognitive Case Studies.* New York: Oxford University Press, 1989.

Keegan, R. T. "Getting Started: Charles Darwin's Early Steps Toward a Creative Life in Science." *Journal of Adult Development,* in press.

Keegan, R. T., and Gruber, H. E. "Commentary." *Human Development,* 1994, 37 (2), 103–108.

Kuper, A. *The Chosen Primate: Human Nature and Cultural Diversity.* Cambridge, Mass.: Harvard University Press, 1994.

Osowski, J. "Ensembles of Metaphor in the Psychology of William James." In D. B. Wallace and H. E. Gruber (eds.), *Creative People at Work: Twelve Cognitive Case Studies.* New York: Oxford University Press, 1989.

Pariser, D. "Normal and Unusual Aspects of Juvenile Artistic Development in Klee, Lautrec, and Picasso." *Creativity Research Journal,* 1991, 4 (1), 51–65.

Piaget, J. *The Child and Reality.* New York: Penguin, 1976.

Schwartz, A. "Recurrence of Things Past: An Exploration of Repetition in Artistic Creativity in Theory and in the Work of Salvador Dali." Unpublished doctoral dissertation, Department of Psychology, Widener University, 1993.

Wallace, D. B., Franklin, M. B., and Keegan, R. T. "The Observing Eye: A Century of Baby Diaries." *Human Development,* 1994, 37 (1), 1–29.

Wallace, D. B., and Gruber, H. E. (eds.). *Creative People at Work: Twelve Cognitive Case Studies.* New York: Oxford University Press, 1989.

Weisberg, R. W. *Creativity: Beyond the Myth of Genius.* New York: Freeman, 1993.

ROBERT T. KEEGAN *is professor of psychology at Pace University in Pleasantville, New York.*

We may unfortunately resist, devalue, and frankly pathologize
divergent and creative thought—all the more worrisome now
in a world requiring increasing awareness and creative flexibility.

Beyond Piaget: Accepting Divergent, Chaotic, and Creative Thought

Ruth Richards

Accept divergent and creative thought? This sounds fine, perhaps, but we are not here to romanticize whatever a young child does, or wants to do. This is, after all, reality.

Here you are one morning, a hassled parent, on the way to work, late (of course) as you exit the door, and bringing in tow this delightful little preschooler who wants to stop and look at everything and do everything with total absorption, and not a care in the world. Never mind the realities of schedules, school times, work obligations. You perhaps threaten a bit with a timeworn, "I'm going to count to three—" or, "If you don't get in the car—" You begin to feel like a drill sergeant, a mistreater of children.

And now this child is wandering off across the back yard lawn, in irregular absentminded steps—a little dreamwalker, a hypnotizee. "Where's that bird going in the grass? I'm going to follow it. Look, there's a hole in the fence. What's behind that hole in the fence. *What is behind that hole in the fence?* I've *got* to know. It could be *anything*. I've never seen out there before. I can look through that hole. Then I can see it. I've *got* to see it. Maybe it's scary, maybe it's a *dinosaur*. Maybe it's a baby T. Rex, a *meat eater*. It's going to be kicking and trying to get out of there. I'm going to go see it and I'll tell it 'hi.' Then I'll run in the house and say 'mommy mommy.'"

Here is a mystery, an obsession, even some magic—and it is the most important problem in the world. The entreaties of the parent are far in the distance.

Now what does a parent do? The focus here isn't on setting limits, but in truth, a child simply can't do whatever she or he wants. Without limits, these kids would never develop the self-discipline to use their creativity. Not to mention that the adults might never make it through the day.

But at a more subtle level, when you look at this kind of scene, don't you sometimes feel just a twinge of discomfort, just a bit at times, that in a different way, things are going too far? That this child is acting just a little too odd, or uncontrolled, or out of touch with reality? And do you ever fear, in an instant about-face, that maybe it's you who are missing the boat? That there's something magical going on here that you have forgotten how to see?

Creativity, Play, and Nonconformity

A great deal has been written about the fantasy play of children. The conclusion, of course, is that fantasy can be fine, it's part of play, and play is the child's work (for example, Ayman-Nolley, 1992; Piaget, 1962; Russ, 1993; Scales, Almy, Nicolopoulou, and Ervin-Tripp, 1991; Smolucha, 1992a, 1992b; Van Hoorn, Nourot, Scales, and Alward, 1993). Play may indeed be viewed as the "cornerstone of imagination" (Van Hoorn, Nourot, Scales, and Alward, 1993, p. 25). Play, furthermore, can help a child adapt to a changing modern world, through a valuing of curiosity, and the exploration of alternative situations.

In addition—and this is key—it appears that children who engage in a lot of make-believe are happier and more flexible when faced with new life situations (Singer and Singer, in Van Hoorn, Nourot, Scales, and Alward, 1993.) Indeed, these children may be happier in general. In the visual arts, for instance, it may be crucial that preschoolers avoid set schemas and create their own structures—and not only that, but create multiple and different structures. Indeed, "The more *diversity*, the more enjoyment a child derives" (de Uriarte, 1978, p. 27). Further, these children may express themselves wholeheartedly with the integrated creativity of their being, telling stories about a picture, dancing to an image—without making the distinctions of medium and expression we may later codify and come to expect (de Uriarte, 1978; personal communication, 1994).

Freedom, self-discovery, discovery of world and one's ability to act in it. Sounds fine. But there is also a well-known price for the adult who works with such creative children. These kids will not always behave in ways an adult might predict or prefer. Consider various reports of creative children who seem difficult, disruptive in class, headstrong at home, in conflict with parents, or isolative or withdrawn (for example, Albert and Runco, 1986; Colangelo and Dettmann, 1983; Dewing, 1970; Getzels and Jackson, 1962; Richards, 1981; Torrance and Myers, 1972; Wallach, 1970).

Although teachers more accepting of creativity can be found (for example, Runco, Johnson, and Bear, 1993), some teachers say they value creativity but, at the same time, devalue certain associated behaviors; indeed, teachers may not even acknowledge the relevance of these behaviors to creativity (for example, see Runco and Okuda, in press; Westby and Dawson, 1995). A more rejecting view yet is found in Getzels and Jackson's (1962) classic study at the secondary school level. These students, incidentally, had an average IQ of 132, such that the group differences may have been more attributable to differences in creativity than to what might be called general intelligence.

Getzels and Jackson found that teachers preferred students who were higher IQ (and lower creativity), to those of higher creativity (and lower IQ). Why was this? Alert, bright, agreeable, cooperative, dutiful, assignments in on time, sit quietly in class, model student, good citizen? In fact, there was strong positive rank order agreement between the personal traits preferred by high-IQ students and those traits they believed teachers preferred. For highly creative students, the picture was different altogether: the correlation was negative. Recent results (Westby and Dawson, 1995) show once again that teachers may link more cooperative and conventional student profiles with creativity.

Given this, and if one assumes that a somewhat difficult behavior pattern among creative young people is normal—or at least is a normal response to family or social pressures against a developing nonconformist—then have we solved our problem? Should one let the wandering and fantasizing preschooler go ahead and imagine, as long as the child gets certain jobs done, and meets certain obligations on time?

There appears to be more to it than that. Even when we understand all the factors thus far discussed, we may not at all times value fantasy and imagination as much as we think we do.

The Illusion of Abnormality

A key article in *American Psychologist* (Shedler, Mayman, and Manis, 1993) looked at psychopathology that can be missed in assessment. Certain disturbed but well-defended individuals are able to hide their pathology on standard mental health scales. One can turn the issue around, and ask instead about behaviors that may be called pathological when they are not.

The question is whether the suspicion of pathology (that is, of a problem adversely affecting health and well-being) may arise precisely because of a person's *lack* of defensiveness, and openness to a range of mental states and processes, along with a nonconformist divergence from what is considered usual, or normal (see also Albert, in press; Richards, 1994). To address this, it is important first to define creativity and then look at potential patterns of innovation and its acceptance at both an individual and societal level of analysis.

Everyday Creativity, Health, and Survival

The present definition of everyday creativity (see Richards and others, 1988; Richards, 1990, in press *c*) is based, significantly, in arguments of health and evolutionary advantage. In the broadest, most everyday sense, creative response helps us adapt to changing environments and conditions; in the extreme case, it helps us survive. It is supported by reports of a temperamental orientation toward unexpected and original response, what Barron (1969) has called a "disposition toward originality," and has been reported in highly creative individuals across fields. Indeed, there may be a real taste for this originality, if not at times even a variant of a possible "addiction" (see Richards, in press *c*)— and this can reveal itself in a variety of activities of everyday life.

Our definition is therefore not an exclusivist one involving only traditional fields of the arts and sciences, for instance, or only socially recognized accomplishment. If survival itself can be at stake, virtually everything must be fair game—must be subject to an inclination or disposition toward originality (Barron, 1969).

We thus consider as creative all real-life outcomes that meet criteria of *originality* and *meaningfulness to others* (after Barron, see Richards and others, 1988), including many variegated activities of everyday life, such as office management, teaching, report writing, child rearing, automobile repairs, team sports, or gourmet cooking. It is not the task itself that ensures its creativity but how the task is done. Many of us have probably had our cars repaired by people representing one extreme of creativity or the other.

Also relevant to the generality of creative styles, it sometimes happens that certain mood disorders in individuals and in families involving an underlying vulnerability for bipolar mood disorders are linked with heightened creativity (for example, see Andreasen, 1987; Jamison, 1990; Ludwig, 1992; Richards and others, 1988; Richards, Kinney, Daniels, and Linkins, 1992; Richards, 1990, 1994). This heightened creativity even includes relatives who are not clinically ill. Significantly, the fields of these persons can be quite different, one from another.

Indeed, an evolutionary advantage has been proposed as the reason for persistence of such otherwise debilitating disorders of mood down through the generations (Richards, 1981; Richards and others, 1988; D. Wilson, 1992). This represents yet another reasons to think a creative advantage may be generalized and not useful only in the arts, or in making music, say, or in a scientific laboratory.

Notably, this creative advantage can even appear across diverse areas, all within the same family. This is not to say that special and distinguishable talents—verbal, visual, and so on—may not be necessary for creativity (for example, see Gardner, 1983; Richards, 1994; Richards and Kinney, 1990). But these may potentially be separated from the originality of their application, again perhaps speaking to a "disposition toward originality" (Barron, 1969). It is one thing to make a perfect copy of a Leonardo da Vinci painting, and another thing entirely to be Leonardo.

Creative Divergence, Chaotic Amplification, and the Evolution of Information

It has been suggested that the *creativity* involved in generating new information may in itself represent a separate yet crucially interlocking strand of evolution (Richards, in press *c*). Comparable to the evolution of genes, one may speak of an ongoing evolution of *memes* (or units of "cultural imitation"; see Dawkins, 1976; Csikszentmihalyi, 1988; Richards, 1990)—of *an evolution of information* (Richards, in press). This informational and cultural process is distinct from biological evolution but can interact readily with it (for example, consider the people who didn't freeze because they discovered how to use fire). As with genetic recombination in mating, *memetic recombination* occurs widely— but can happen in greatly more complex ways, since it can, literally, draw all at once on information spanning millions of miles and millions of years. Indeed, the most abundant and fertile forms of new information will, in general, tend to be the most creative ones. Further, in a world of information, the complexity of creative forms will continue to increase dramatically as a result of a widespread, incessant, and densely interconnected use by many millions of persons alive on this planet.

As we are increasingly aware (for example, E. O. Wilson, 1992, 1993), the chance of our biological survival as a species is enhanced by the diversity of our genotypes and related phenotypes—by our underlying genetic material, and the spectrum of real-life ways in which this can be expressed across differing environments. Similarly, our biological as well as cultural survival is surely enhanced by this proliferation of diverse ideas and information. And just as surely as the species of the earth should be respectfully preserved, so should this richness of mental creation. A potential advantage should lie in a cultural process that continues to generate new mental products, including creation of some wild or way-out thoughts and notions, along with more conservative ones.

Next, if such gems of creative divergence are the substrate, chaotic mental processes may be the amplifier. At minimum, chaotic phenomena can be proposed as both model and metaphor for creative insight. The process of *creative insight*—the so-called aha experience—may at times conceivably resemble an *edge-of-chaos* phenomenon (see Richards, in press *a,* in press *c*). As metaphor, consider the famed butterfly whose flapping wing in Peking can cause a storm system to erupt over New York—the so-called Butterfly Effect (Gleick, 1987). Certain weather conditions represent a precariously balanced system that can fall suddenly into a new order; it can be dramatically responsive, even to minute forms of input. Think of the final snowflake that precedes an avalanche (Bak and Chen, 1991), launching the catastrophic event.

Generally speaking, large systems built from simple interacting elements tend to move toward their own *emergent structure* (Forrest, 1991). As with the preavalanche snowfall, or prestorm weather system, small changes can accrue, perhaps slowly and quietly, interacting locally, yet evolving an expanding and massive structure of interdependence and sensitivity—evolving ultimately toward a chaotic state. At this point, even minute changes in initial conditions may bring about widespread response (Bak and Chen, 1991; Forrest, 1991, Gleick, 1987).

One may translate this to a context of mental change and transformation. Forrest (1991), speaking of emergent structures in modeling intelligent human behavior, concluded that "this may be the only feasible method" (p. 1). There are indeed increasingly frequent reports of chaotic phenomena in human physiology (see Krippner, 1994), including characteristic EEG patterns that appear to collapse from a chaotic background state during the mental processing of new odors (Skarda and Freeman, 1987). It is quite plausible that, with creativity, key new information, sometimes even trivial sounding in itself, could trigger a cascade of mental changes and reorganizations, even at times a major paradigm shift (Richards, in press *a*, in press *c*). Here indeed may be the creative insight. (Or, on a bad day, the last mental straw.)

Thus may be born one's first glimpses of the likes of radioactivity, double-stranded DNA, or the concept of the unconscious. Perhaps it is the wisdom of nature that certain mental shifts may, for all of us, come relatively unbidden and unforeseen. How clever to have such a built-in mechanism to destabilize, reorganize, and kick us out of our mental ruts.

Yet not all new ideas will be good, or even passable. For each hit that is generated, there may be in society a range of near misses, and these need to be sorted out in turn by other societal forces, such as teachers, parents, editors, bosses, critics. (Piaget, interestingly, addressed a similar notion at the societal level; see Labouvie-Vief, 1980). We have referred to this underlying dialectic as *cultural brainstorming* (Richards, in press *a*, in press *c*). It should take place at the local and interpersonal level, as well as the level of major societal innovation.

But how does one balance conservatism and innovation, at the individual or societal level? And when might the balance need to be changed?

Is It Thought Disorder? (Adults). Along with a sometimes very reactive (and potentially chaotic) response system for creative mental processing, we postulate a generator of small mental changes, emitting highly original input from time to time, which could start the larger ball rolling. Here is the rest of the proposed mechanism to destabilize, reorganize, and kick us out of our mental ruts.

The discussion begins first of all with adults, and then moves to the special case of children. The question to many would be whether the following adults might be considered psychiatrically ill. Responses follow to some Rorschach-type inkblots on The Thought Disorder Index (Holzman, Shenton, and Solovay, 1986; Shenton and others, 1989). The responses, at least, were considered "thought disordered" (Solovay and others, 1986; see Richards, 1994):

Two potatoes with eyes and a mouth trying to climb up some kind of pipe or pole.
A witch on a broom stick. And it looked like an electric broom stick or something . . . gas powered because she had a cloud of smoke.
It's black, dark, darkness, lovemaking.

There's not much to go on here, although respondents were indeed psychiatric patients, and showed forms of thought disorder often associated with mania (Holzman, Shenton, and Solovay, 1986). A fanciful quality is present that one might find appealing in a different context. The last interpretation, for instance, could be evocative in a poem. One may certainly think of the emerging connections between bipolar disorders and creativity (for example, Andreasen, 1987; Andreasen and Canter, 1974; Andreasen and Powers, 1974; Jamison, 1990; Ludwig, 1992; Richards, 1981, 1994, in press c). Significantly, qualitatively similar "thought disorder" has also shown up in more muted form in patients' relatives who were not, themselves, clinically ill (Shenton and others, 1989). Thus, it is not pathology or suffering but something much more subtle that may be making the difference.

It is also worth noting other instances of *abnormal* (unusual) response that isn't necessarily *ill* (maladaptive). Included are Eysenck's (1993) findings of elevated "psychoticism" among high scorers on tests of creativity, and Schuldberg's reports of unusual perceptual experiences and beliefs. Barron and associates (Barron, 1969) found high MMPI psychopathology scores for eminent creators across several fields. Indeed the average creative writer was in the top 15 percent of the general population on *every* such scale, a finding that was ascribed in part to greater psychological openness. Eminent writers also showed a high level of overinclusive conceptualization in Andreasen and Canter's (1974) research. However, creators in both Barron and Schuldberg's work also showed high levels of "ego strength," and Andreasen and Canter's writers, when compared to manic patients, showed advantages in abstract and cohesive thinking (see Andreasen and Powers, 1974; also Richards, 1994, in press).

Looking beyond findings of increased creativity and a personal or family history of bipolar disorders, it is central that—for all of us—even slight elevations of mood can lead directly to some of these very same patterns, including more unusual word associations, overinclusive categorization, and enhanced creative problem solving (Richards, 1993a, 1994, in press c).

Hence, one may wish to distinguish Kris's (1951) creative "regression in the service of the ego" from a less intentional and more pathological "regression" to more "primitive" forms of thought. It isn't the response per se that necessarily determines creativity versus pathology, but the reason the response is given. (With the young child, the details of this intentionality may at times be mysterious; yet there is still some semblance of purpose, of conscious exploration, and of control.) Use of such distinctions may lead to a broader and more complex picture of the normal range of human functioning.

Comparing Creative Thinking Test Results. The point can be highlighted by comparing two sets of responses to a divergent thinking test item, such as was pioneered by Guilford or Torrance (see Richards, 1981; Torrance and Myers, 1972; Wallach, 1970), "List all the uses you can think of for a pencil." One person says a pencil can be used for writing a letter, a note, or a postcard. A second person says it can be used for a backscratcher, a potting stake, kindling for a fire, a rolling pin for baking, a toy for a woodpecker, or a small boat for a cricket. The second person gets higher points for originality.

But—"a small boat for a cricket?" Isn't this getting rather far-fetched? Of course, this is precisely the point in sessions of brainstorming (Osborn, 1963). To use up the more common ideas, pull in some more bizarre ones (at first without criticism) and then later sort and choose among these. But just watch out if one tries to do this in the wrong context. Proposing a boat for a cricket would be a good candidate for a diagnosis of thought disorder.

Finally, one should note this is not a challenge to the entire notion of thought disorder. We are only asking why specific thoughts should inevitably be called disordered. By contrast, one can compare two other inkblot responses that are arguably less useful or creative (Solovay and others, 1986). Without reference to the actual stimulus ink blots, these interpretations still seem less thoughtful, deliberate, and integrated, and more idiosyncratic and potentially out of touch with the real task requirements. We return to our two criteria for creative response, originality and meaningfulness. If parts of the following are *original*, they will not, to an impartial observer, necessarily be as *meaningful*:

A masquerade party costume. Cha cha. Clap hands. Let's dance.
A crab. . . . 'cause I'm Cancer the Crab maybe. My sign is Cancer. My horo-
    scope. And I'm thinking a lot about cancer too.

Is It Thought Disorder? (Young Children). A preschooler may say a broomstick is a horse, or a couch is an airplane. These fantasies may be fixed to the concrete objects. In fact, if someone pulls away the broomstick, the ride is probably over. Further, in Piaget's (1962) terms, in symbolic play, there is a primacy of *assimilation* to *accommodation*. There is much more fitting of new environmental input to existing mental structures than altering of those mental structures to fit with new data. These functions of assimilation and accommodation are not yet in balance—which is Piaget's condition for *adaptation* (for example, see Flavell, 1963). Things are enjoyably egocentric, and very wish-fulfilling. In fantasy, the thing becomes what one wants it to be. In the example of the child riding a horse, the broomstickness of the object counts very little—at least compared to how fast it will go!

Now surely this is not thought disorder.

It will be some years before these kids can bring the power of abstract thinking to their drama and put away the props, as well as figure out (and perhaps care to figure out) how much sense this drama makes in reality (for example, see Ayman-Nolley, 1992; Piaget, 1962; Smolucha, 1992a, 1992b). The preschoolers' manipulations are concrete, real, and present. But then again, that is the nature of their job.

And this job *is* creative—it is original, deliberate, and meaningful to others (meaningful, at least—and here we qualify a bit, regarding the young child—it is *meaningful* within the child's own developing world, as understood here by the child, along with perhaps a sensitive parent or teacher). Despite what looks like idiosyncrasy, at times, the social and communicative aspects of the child's productions are also becoming increasingly well recognized (Scales, Almy, Nicolopoulou, and Ervin-Tripp, 1991; Smolucha, 1992a, 1992b).

Yet if one does not take into account the various developmental differences in growing children, such childish productions and preoccupations
might at times seem abnormal and even alarming. They may seem so different
from what adults usually experience—or at least what adults experience consciously. In the next section, we look at two sorts of examples of this.

Are Primitive Conceptual Modes One Key to Creativity?

Just what is a broomstick, anyway? Young children form concepts in their own
characteristic ways. From the beginning of symbolic representation to approximately four or five years of age, according to Piaget (1962), children form *preconcepts*. These have neither generality (as in a hierarchy of categories, nesting
one inside the other, for example, red and green blocks), nor true individual-
ity (where an object has a fixed identity or constancy outside the field of action
or comparison).

Both assimilation and accommodation are at work, but in shaky and
incomplete ways. For instance, a new block (for example, a red one), can be
assimilated or linked to one member of a set (for example, another red block),
which in the child's mind stands for the whole set, with any differences over-
looked (for example, a set of red and green and purple blocks). The red block
is not seen as one among many. Accommodation, too, can be thus centered
within a set, rather than encompassing the whole. A blue block arrives, and
now there are blue and red blocks. (Forget the green and purple ones.) The
child's notion of generality is still in the future.

Yet kids do learn, and as they approach adolescence, their concepts look
more and more like our own concepts, and more and more like each other's.
In this sense, concepts increasingly serve a social and cultural function (Vygotsky, 1986). The other modes may seem to disappear, or at least to be driven
underground (see Richards, 1981).

But are these previous modes now destined to be forgotten? Not necessarily. What surprises, what fun, and what new insights can now be produced by
a return to these earlier modes of thinking—now functioning as bold destabi-
lizing forces—when integrated with a more mature and socially consensual edit-
ing function. Kekule dreamed that he was a snake biting his tail, which led to
discovery of the benzene ring, a key concept in organic chemistry (Arieti, 1976).
When he processed this notion, Kekule did not really think he was a snake. Nor
did he think that a benzene ring had a tail. But the combination of images was
sufficient to produce a key chemical insight at the highest level of abstraction.

For further elaboration, we turn to Vygotsky's (1986) experimental delin-
eation of five forms of *thinking in complexes,* characteristic of the young child.
This scheme is detailed, graphic, and the result of extensive study of early concept formation.

How does a child begin? Syncretic conglomerations. Once children have some
command of a language—a way of symbolizing things—they can increasingly
find meanings that unite things, and make more sense of the world around

them. A crazy jumble of sensations begins to fall out into more organized patterns. Through grouping and naming, children learn to see much more, and to master much more of their world. In sorting objects, some initial "heaps" or "syncretic conglomerations" described by Vygotsky (1986), based on vague subjective bonds, include groupings formed by *trial and error,* and based on simple *contiguity in space.*

Thinking in complexes. Vygotsky (1986) described the next stage as thinking in "family names," where experimental groupings take on an umbrella identity, although there is no necessary unity connecting all members. There are five stages: *association by similarity* (with shifting criteria linking new members to a single nuclear object, for example, redness, triangularity, spatial proximity), *association by contrast* (not red, not round), the *chain complex* (a dynamic ongoing joining, for example, red block, green block, green circle, yellow circle), *diffuse complex* (where criteria can be unstably shifting, for example, from triangle to trapezoid, or from blue to green—nonetheless, a tenuous connecting pattern is beginning to emerge), and the *pseudoconcept* (which looks like a concept, for example, they are all yellow triangles; however, except that each pair was formed concretely and individually and is really a fancy association complex).

Further examples, with the association complex, and chain complex. Some primitive groupings can be delightful. Take, for instance, a toddler who thought a chain saw was a cow (it made the right noise). Also identified cheerfully as a cow was a black-and-white patterned fish at the aquarium (it had the right colorings), and a familiar farm animal that gives milk (see Richards, in press *c*).

A chain complex, here, might look more like a string of loose associations. The child starts with a black-and-white cow and begins to find things that go together. Now here's a cow that's black, and a horse that's black, and a little boy who sits on the horse, and another figure, a little girl this time, and here's a house (and now the figures go inside, but the child bumps the house in doing this), and here's some shaking of the house (now the child rattles it on purpose), and now the chimney falls off, but here's a block that's the same shape as the chimney (the child puts it in the house for safekeeping, along with the chimney), and claps his hands. There! he says, delighted.

There are elements above of a *thematic,* or story telling, grouping (see Richards, 1981), as well, so this is not a pure example. Plus we don't want to force-fit the following point. But it is worth considering the similarity of some of these primitive conceptual schemes or complexes to (1) the unusual associations and overinclusive forms of categorization characteristic of highly creative people (Andreasen and Powers, 1975; Richards, 1993b, 1994); (2) the comparable findings on persons at risk for bipolar mood disorders (Andreasen and Canter, 1974; Jamison, 1990; Richards, 1993b, 1994) and for other pathologies (Eysenck, 1993); (3) the relevant forms of loose or combinatory thought disorder found during "highs" in bipolar individuals (Holzman, Shenton, and Solovay, 1986; Solovay and others, 1986); and finally, in (4) the unusual associations and overinclusion evoked by conditions of mild mood elevation in the population at large.

Relation to primary process thinking. Might there also be, for all of us, some relation to the so-called formal and ongoing characteristics of Freud's primary process thought? These formal properties were characterized by Holt (in Russ, 1993) as "illogical thinking, condensation (fusion of two ideas or images), and loose, associative links" (p. 18). Primary process thought has been viewed by individuals including Arieti, Holt, Suler, and Lazarus as possessing its own structures, development, and running separately and perhaps parallel to Freud's more reality-oriented secondary process (see Russ, 1993). Its creative potential is said to be available, as mentioned, through the process of "regression in the service of the ego" (Kris, 1951).

Russ (1993) emphasizes the intense importance of affect to primary process thought, proposing that primary process involves "material around which the child had experienced early intense feeling states (oral, anal, aggressive). Current primary process content may reflect either current affect or a kind of 'affective residue' in cognition left over from earlier developmental stages" (p. 19). She notes how primary process can contribute to a cognitive style or stylistic way of dealing with affective material.

This emphasis is important, and stands in contrast to Piaget (1981), who saw affect as less directive and more as a secondary force energizing cognitive processing. Yet in expanding one's own viewpoint, one should also consider moving beyond an instinctual drive model for creativity (for example, Freud [1908] 1958) to encompass a greater and more humanistic range of interests and motivating forces—including a drive for mastery, curiosity, wonder, and awe (see Krippner, 1994; Richards, 1981, 1990). In the fullest experiencing of life's possibilities should lie the richest mental palette for creativity.

Integrating modes of thought. Now it may be proposed, more generally, that creative states in adults include an altered state of consciousness with a strong *affective* coloration that increases mental connectivity in a free-flowing way. This may be far from Piaget's perfect equilibrium of formal conceptual thought, with its perfect balance of assimilation and accommodation, of adaptation, and mental operations that are predictable, reversible, universal, and consensually employed.

Here is idiosyncrasy, egocentricity, assimilation over accommodation, and a direction that can not necessarily even be imagined, never mind reversed. It may at times even conceivably be a road to a mental edge of chaos, where a key piece of data can destabilize and reorganize an entire mental substructure of cumulative and interacting understandings. From the subjective end, this may bring the experience of creative insight. There is a sensitive dependence upon initial conditions (for example, see Feigenbaum, in Peitgen, Jurgens, and Saupe, 1992; Gleick, 1987). Indeed, a desired result of a program such as Gordon's Synectics (1961) is to elaborate sudden new insights through the introduction of unlikely analogies.

In this case, we no longer have a struggling child pursuing such creative goals, but an adult who can in addition bring the whole Piagetian armamentarium to bear. This adult can put on the formal conceptual brakes, and use the new insight in a way that is not only original, but, as we have said in defining creativity, also meaningful to others.

Indeed, there is evidence that certain so-called primitive modes of thought never actually do disappear, but remain latent in the older person. In adolescence, in the best case, according to Vygotsky (in Smolucha, 1992a, p. 56), "Imagination has become a higher mental function as a result of the influence of inner speech, and collaborates with thinking in concepts to form a psychological system that organizes creative thinking." Hence the highly creative person comes to develop a "flexible access to conceptual styles of different developmental origin" (Richards, 1981).

Example of More Primitive Process: In the Forest

Our memories, after all, aren't organized according to stringent rules of logic. Mentally, we live in a richly interconnected world of associations. It is a dense neural forest, an ecology of thought and memory. Here, each new exposure can reverberate deeply within prior experience.

Let us stay with the forest a minute. Make it a redwood forest, tall sequoias to the heavens, dense ground beneath, cool, wet, stray beams of sunlight flickering through tall boughs, hanging moss, the ground matted with needles, cones, brush, ground ferns, trails of soft slimy creatures. You stop, you listen to the silence. Not even the distant traffic is heard, so usual that its absence is thundering. The song of a bird, the drop of high moisture, and then everything is still. One is enclosed, enwombed, in a forest that exceeds one's own scale even to imagine, one's mightiest parent, so comforting and natural that, indeed, one might always have been there.

Associating Through a Forest—The Content. How does one see this forest? It's not a sensory snapshot, taken verbatim, to be filed away. It is processed by its own creative process, in conjunction with everything related and remembered in one's past. It is linked to a web of prior experience by its most salient subjective points in a way that is richly complex, and that can be accessed later in any number of different ways.

There are the stories about the forest you once heard, the summer trip with your family, the drives with your grandfather, the walks with your mother, the picture books, the postcards from friends, the forest scenes in *Star Wars,* a two-week summer camp, the smell of a gift soap from a friend, the special night of one of your first dates. You may not consciously summon up all this history. You may not even summon up its feelings. You might not even be able to remember it consciously if you wanted to. But, somehow, it is all there.

Perhaps even deeper longings join as well, ones common to us all as a species, and that also lie latent in our mental structures. E. O. Wilson (1992) asks why we go to such trouble to plant those trees in the yard, to visit the forests and national parks and stand and gaze in wonder. Why would so many of us go to so much trouble? Perhaps because this fulfills an ancient yearning, a *biophilia,* a need to connect with the rest of organic nature, and to be home.

Associating Through a Forest—The Process. Now look at how these associations have formed, even below our awareness in the depths of the mind. We've gone beyond concepts and logic. We are swimming from oceans to grandmas to camping trips and walking slowly down a sunlit lane. These memories are borne on the tides of our feelings, and on the links of the most primitive of types of complexes and syncretic ties. Yet somehow these all connect, and so intimately and well.

One can indeed regress to an earlier level of development, and indeed to an altered state of consciousness, and mentally swim most freely among the myriad content that is there. In this way, one can forge new connections that might never have arisen if one had stayed on the road and taken the well-traveled highways of concepts and structures and topic outlines. Down here, in the primordial soup, one sees the snake bite its tail, and there is Kekule's concept of the benzene ring—six carbon atoms in a ringlike structure—shining through one's dream and heralding the basis for all of organic chemistry.

Winnowing of Cognitive Styles and the Risks of Habituation

Sooner or later, children find out how they're "supposed to" be doing these concept formation tasks. For instance, to reflect an earlier example, *cow* is found to be the name of a class of living creatures with all (more or less) of a set of attributes. A particular one of these attributes does not, in itself, signify cow. Indeed, a moo is not a cow. Not even if a cow is doing the mooing. Most certainly not if a chain saw is doing the mooing.

Interestingly, this is also a point of the present chapter. Certain utterances, one may say, are not in themselves necessarily disordered or sick. It depends, once again, on the context or big picture. Thus, one duly may come to apply a higher level of abstract conceptualization to the assessment of psychopathology.

Analytic and Inferential Thinking. And what is the conceptual goal at the end of the tunnel—the concepts that may make a teacher or parent's eyes shine? At the adolescent level, these include analytic-descriptive (common attribute) and inferential-categorical (superordinate class) bases. In the first, or analytic, case, we might have "things that are red," "things that smell like cinnamon," or "things that float in water but not in oil."

In the second case, one may have classes of objects that all could be called *balls, cars,* or *cities.* Or creatures called *lions, elephants,* or *dolphins.* Each grouping is defined by certain key features. In the case of a defined species such as *Tursiops truncatus* (the bottle-nosed dolphin), these features are extremely specific. Likewise for our own membership group, *human beings.* But there are much more slippery concepts as well, including abstract qualities such as *altruism, friendship,* or *betrayal.* Here the qualities leading to each inference can be especially illusory, subjective, culture-bound, changeable and, most certainly, debatable.

A Richer Verbal Palette. As mentioned, when some children get the knack of this abstract (analytic and inferential) thinking, they can come to forget some of their earlier and perhaps fumbling attempts. If not valued in the environment, their more primitive styles of thinking can go underground (Richards, 1981). This happens for many young people, at least. But not for certain creative people. Not only can they still access earlier modes, they still want to access them. Now they also know what they're doing—they may even think about this consciously—and now their reasons for calling on more primitive thought patterns will be different from when they were younger. They have a richer range of available cognitive styles and, this time, are truly painting with a richer palette. (See also Smolucha, 1ᵒ92a, 1992b).

And what about the rest? Vygotsky (in Smolucha, 1992a) noted two extreme patterns: one, as noted, in which imagination continued onward as reason ascends, and one in which it curves down like an arrow that has reached the top of its parabola of flight. Vygotsky's overall viewpoint was discouraging: "The majority of people go little by little to the prosaic side of practical life, conceal the dreams of their youth, consider love a chimera, etc. This, however, is only a regression but not an elimination" (p. 55).

Mechanisms to Open Minds and Seed Change. There are other ways, certainly, to free up one's colorful mental processes and generate a diversity of creative response beyond, say, drawing on a personal or family history of a mood disorder and its potential for divergent thought (assuming this even works). There are many routes to creativity (Richards, 1981, 1990). In theory, anyone can choose to keep, develop, and integrate—as well as to help others develop—a richer program of mental options. Doing so involves strategies of metacognition, as well as meta metacognition, levels of thinking about how we think—and indeed of thinking about how we think about it. Kitchener (1983) has described just such higher levels of cognition, going beyond a framework such as Piaget's. This type of mental reflection and development might alternatively be seen as part of our "conscious evolution" as a species (see Ornstein and Ehrlich, 1989; Richards, 1993a, 1993b, in press *c*). But we will return for a moment to mood disorders and their significance. The question does indeed arise (see Richards, in press *c*) as to whether the high population rates of bipolar spectrum mood disorders—even perhaps as high as 4 percent to 5 percent (Akiskal and Akiskal, 1992; Akiskal and Mallya, 1987)—is related to a particular *cognitive niche* (Tooby and DeVore, 1987) that is somehow filled. Within the diversity of individuals in society, this subpopulation could help guarantee a quantity of *instigators,* persons with radical ideas to help seed change, at both the personal and societal level (Richards, in press *a*, in press *c*). D. Wilson (1992) indicates that the genes for bipolar disorder prevail at *five hundred times* the adjusted mutation equilibrium rate. This suggests that the phenomenon is anything but a chance one.

There are, one should note, several issues. People at risk for bipolar disorders show positive, creativity-enhancing behaviors that may be *pathologized*. Among persons who may be stigmatized, notably, are a large number of children at risk. Meanwhile, many of the associated creative behaviors may not only be healthy for individuals (see Richards, 1990, 1994, in press *c*), but for society at large. To make matters worse, we also find other people with similar creative behaviors who may be stigmatized by association with this first underappreciated group. Thus, we have mistaken notions of thought disorder and the like. Finally, in a world of increasing threat and decreasing space and resources (for example, see Richards 1993b, Brown and others, 1992; Gruber, 1989; Ornstein and Ehrlich, 1989) we need more, not fewer, of these creative instigators. We therefore badly need to *expand our acceptable limits of normality* to take full advantage of the rich potential available within every segment of our society (Albert, in press; Richards, in press)—and indeed within each one of us.

The Risks of Habituation. As we are all aware, the young child often has a much richer experience than we do. Think of the amazing freshness that confronts the inexperienced mind. We adults have truly "seen it all before." And so, old fogies that we are, we have ceased to see it. We habituate to repetition, even of great beauty—be this the same old route to work ("oh, these narrow seaside roads are really slowing me down"), or the beauty of the spring flowers ("I don't believe it—it's already time to mow!"). Only the immediate need for action (getting to one's job; doing the chores) will at times bring these surroundings to awareness.

Yet this is not our experience, nor do we expect it to be, if we go to visit a distant country, or confront some other radically different experience. We are there precisely to have the experience. We savor the differences (at least if this is our inclination), and our conscious awareness of them.

At other times, our formal concepts, which can be so much help, become no help at all. For if we have the world all boxed and packaged, then where is the cause for wonder, never mind attention? If we assimilate everything to our rules and categories, then that is that. In addition, our minds have evolved the efficient strategy of ignoring the habitual, the routine and commonplace—whether what we see (Richards, 1993a, 1993b) or feel (Frijda, 1988). It is changes, edges, movement, or surprise that we react to. We have evolved to detect the lion that is about to pounce, and not to question whether to drive to work a different way on the two-hundredth day of the year.

Indeed, we are even blind enough, in an evolutionary sense, to overlook a steadily increasing lethal danger—and there are many examples in our world, including population expansion, atmospheric poisons, and disease (Gruber, 1989; Ornstein and Ehrlich, 1989; Richards, 1993a, 1993b).

The child: awareness, beauty, and survival—the ocean as example. From an evolutionary point of view, the young child at least may be doing a little better. She or he is still reacting to novelty. The child sees the ocean and needs to make its acquaintance (again, see D. Wilson, 1992). The rocks, the spray, the sparkle of sun, the wind in one's face, the noise!, the seagulls, the precipitous drop off a cliff, the ocean steamer in the distance—motionless, but trailing in its wake a line of white.

In this beauty and complexity is perhaps an intrinsic message: Attend! This vista is life-giving, to be revered. Don't just catalogue this one, O Growing Mind, but place it among the deepest repository of memories that will continue to resonate with every other thought.

And so—gently—it is put into its place.

Our aesthetics may, in fact, carry some ultimate messages of survival. Mitchell Feigenbaum, the chaos theorist, expressed a belief in the significance of beauty in the following statement (in Gleick, 1987, pp. 186–187), "I do want to know how to describe clouds. But to say there's a piece over here with that much density, and a piece . . . I think is wrong. . . . it's not how an artist perceives them. . . . writing down partial differential equations. . . . Somehow the wondrous promise of the earth is that there are things beautiful in it, things wondrous and alluring, and by virtue of your trade you want to understand them."

Here, indeed is a message for us as a culture. Many in our society consider science a central intellectual pursuit, and the arts a more expressive, emotional—and often separate and optional—endeavor (Richards, in press b). It is not so. There are many ways to learn. And so much to wake up and *see*. (Also see Feist, 1991; Runco and Shaw, 1994.)

The adult: day-to-day realities. But now here we are again, timeworn and hassled (and with this curious kid in the back seat). We're at the ocean. We already know all about the spray, the rocks, the sun. We've got this under control. But what about that approaching car? How fast should we go? How fast should we take this turn? As with the hunter in the jungle, it is not the beauty of the palm fronds that catches our attention this time. It is the lion about to pounce.

We are each attending to different things, the adult and the child. And for totally different reasons. At times, the child may be seeing much further than we do. If there is pathology this time, perhaps it is our own. Through a focus on conscious cognition (Langer, 1989), mindfulness (Hanh, 1976), and our own "conscious evolution" (Ornstein and Ehrlich, 1989), we can now attend to expanding our own *limits of normality*.

Observing the Observer

Now finally we turn again to ourselves, as arbiters of the normal or abnormal, and of the creative in our young children. What exactly is our problem?

As if the limitations already discussed weren't bad enough, we humans also have an inherent fear of strangers, fear of the group that is not our own, derived from the environment of evolution (for example, Glantz and Pearce, 1989; Richards, in press a, in press c). Thus we may sometimes reject automatically too much divergence or unfamiliarity as a potential threat, before we come to know what it truly means.

In the same context, perhaps, we as well-meaning clinicians or educators can get hung up on the sniffing-out of abnormality. We fail to see highly positive features within debilitating conditions when negativity is at all present (see Glantz and Pearce, 1989; Jamison, 1990; Ornstein and Ehrlich, 1989; Richards, 1990, 1993a; Schuldberg, 1994).

Then finally, there are the realities of time and energy. As individuals and professionals, we are often greatly challenged by honoring the demands of nurturing the unknown and unexpected (that is, the budding creativity) in young children. This task can be difficult and exhausting, and indeed can represent a balancing act between facilitating innovation and testing limits. One needs to know just where one stands on all the other issues to keep perspective at such times.

But the final message is how much we can learn, not only about our children, but about ourselves and our world, by attending to and facilitating the developing child's marvelous modes of thought. There is also a great deal we can reclaim for ourselves in this pursuit. For it is truly by retaining the mind of the child—with all its openness, wonder, sensitivity, and surprise—along with the guiding skills of the adult, that we can create the greatest "evolution of creativity," and the greatest hope for the world of the future.

Finally, I wish to end with a comment from Maureen Chambers, a gifted and concerned preschool teacher: "At the preschool age, children live in the present. They do not have a grasp on the concept of time. They can be furious one minute, and then laughing again before the angry tears have even been wiped away. They have not learned to put on the masks that adults wear. They are intense and forgiving. That is why it's so important to let them feel and think and create now, because at some point, later in life, the walls will go up."

References

Akiskal, H., and Akiskal, K. "Cyclothymic, Hyperthymic, and Depressive Temperaments as Subaffective Variants of Mood Disorders." In A. Tasman and M. B. Riba (eds.), *Review of Psychiatry,* Vol. 11. Washington, D.C.: American Psychiatric Press, 1992.

Akiskal, H., and Mallya, G. "Criteria for the 'Soft' Bipolar Spectrum: Treatment Implications." *Psychopharmacology Bulletin,* 1987, *23,* 68–73.

Albert, R. S. "The Achievement of Eminence as an Evolutionary Strategy." In M. A. Runco (ed.), *Creativity Research Handbook,* Vol. 2. Cresskill, N.J.: Hampton Press, in press.

Albert, R. S., and Runco, M. A. "The Achievement of Eminence." In R. J. Sternberg and J. E. Davidson (eds.), *Conceptions of Giftedness.* New York: Cambridge University Press, 1986.

Andreasen, N. "Creativity and Mental Illness: Prevalence Rates in Writers and Their First-Degree Relatives." *American Journal of Psychiatry,* 1987, *144,* 1288–1292.

Andreasen, N., and Canter, A. "The Creative Writer: Psychiatric Symptoms and Family History." *Comprehensive Psychiatry,* 1974, *15,* 123–131.

Andreasen, N., and Powers, P. "Overinclusive Thinking in Mania and Schizophrenia." *British Journal of Psychiatry,* 1974, *125,* 452–456.

Arieti, S. *Creativity: The Magic Synthesis.* New York: Basic Books, 1976.

Ayman-Nolley, S. "Vygotsky's Perspective on the Development of Imagination and Creativity." *Creativity Research Journal,* 1992, *5,* 77–85.

Bak, P., and Chen, K. "Self-Organized Criticality." *Scientific American,* Jan. 1991, pp. 46–53.

Barron, F. *Creative Person and Creative Process.* Austin, Tex.: Holt, Rinehart and Winston, 1969.

Brown, L. R., and others. *State of the World, 1992: A Worldwatch Institute Report on Progress Toward a Sustainable Society.* New York: Norton, 1992.

Colangelo, N., and Dettmann, D. F. "A Review of Research on Parents and Families of Gifted Children." *Exceptional Children,* 1983, *50,* 20–27.

Csikszentmihalyi, M. "Society, Culture, and Person: A Systems View of Creativity." In R. J. Sternberg (ed.), *The Nature of Creativity.* New York: Cambridge University Press, 1988.

Dawkins, R. *The Selfish Gene.* New York: Oxford University Press, 1976.

de Uriarte, M. "Art Without Interference: Exploring the Aesthetic Instinct." *Berkeley Monthly,* Nov. 2, 1978, pp. 25–28.

Dewing, K. "Family Influences on Creativity: A Review and Discussion." *Journal of Special Education,* 1970, *4,* 399–404.

Eysenck, H. J. "Creativity and Personality: Suggestions for a Theory." *Psychological Inquiry,* 1993, *4,* 147–178.

Feist, G. J. "Synthetic and Analytic Thought: Similarities and Differences Among Art and Science Students." *Creativity Research Journal,* 1991, *4,* 145–155.

Flavell, J. H. *The Developmental Psychology of Jean Piaget.* New York: Van Nostrand Reinhold, 1963.

Forrest, S. "Emergent Computation: Self-Organizing, Collective, and Cooperative Phenomena in Natural and Artificial Computing Networks." In S. Forrest (ed.), *Emergent Computation.* Cambridge, Mass.: MIT Press, 1991.

Freud, S. "The Relation of the Poet to Day-Dreaming." In S. Freud, *On Creativity and the Unconscious.* New York: Random House, 1958. (Originally published 1908.)

Frijda, N. H. "The Laws of Emotion." *American Psychologist,* 1988, *43,* 349–358.

Gardner, H. *Frames of Mind.* New York: Basic Books, 1983.

Getzels, J. W., and Jackson, P. W. *Creativity and Intelligence: Explorations with Gifted Students.* New York: Wiley, 1962.

Glantz, K., and Pearce, J. K. *Exiles from Eden: Psychotherapy from an Evolutionary Perspective.* New York: Norton, 1989.

Gleick, J. *Chaos: Making a New Science.* New York: Penguin, 1987.

Gordon, W. J. *Synectics: The Development of Creative Capacity.* New York: HarperCollins, 1961.

Gruber, H. "Creativity and Human Survival." In D. Wallace and H. Gruber (eds.), *Creative People at Work.* New York: Oxford University Press, 1989.

Hanh, T. N. *The Miracle of Mindfulness.* Boston: Beacon Press, 1976.

Holzman, P. S., Shenton, M. E., and Solovay, M. R. "Quality of Thought Disorder in Differential Diagnosis." *Schizophrenia Bulletin,* 1986, *12,* 360–372.

Jamison, K. R. "Manic-Depressive Illness, Creativity, and Leadership." In F. K. Goodwin and K. R. Jamison (eds.), *Manic-Depressive Illness.* New York: Oxford University Press, 1990.

Kitchener, K. S. "Cognition, Metacognition, and Epistemic Cognition." *Human Development,* 1983, *26,* 222–232.

Krippner, S. "Humanistic Psychology and Chaos Theory: The Third Revolution and the Third Force." *Journal of Humanistic Psychology,* 1994, *34* (3), 48–61.

Kris, E. *Psychoanalytic Explorations in Art.* Madison, Conn.: International Universities Press, 1951.

Labouvie-Vief, G. "Beyond Formal Operations: Uses and Limits of Pure Logic in Life-Span Development." *Human Development,* 1980, *23,* 141–161.

Langer, E. *Mindfulness.* Reading, Mass.: Addison-Wesley, 1989.

Ludwig, A. M. "Creative Achievement and Psychopathology: Comparison Among Professions." *American Journal of Psychotherapy,* 1992, *46,* 330–353.

Ornstein, R., and Ehrlich, P. *New World, New Mind: Moving Toward Conscious Evolution.* New York: Touchstone, 1989.

Osborn, A. F. *Applied Imagination.* New York: Scribner, 1963.

Peitgen, H.-O., Jurgens, H., and Saupe, D. *Chaos and Fractals: New Frontiers of Science.* New York: Springer–Verlag, 1992.

Piaget, J. *Play, Dreams, and Imitation in Childhood.* New York: Norton, 1962.

Piaget, J. *Intelligence and Affectivity: Their Relationship During Child Development.* Palo Alto: Annual Reviews, 1981.

Richards, R. "Relationships Between Creativity and Psychopathology: An Evaluation and Interpretation of the Evidence." *Genetic Psychology Monographs,* 1981, *103,* 261–324.

Richards, R. "Everyday Creativity, Eminent Creativity, and Health: 'Afterview' for CRJ Special Issues on Creativity and Health." *Creativity Research Journal,* 1990, *3,* 300–326.

Richards, R. "Everyday Creativity, Eminent Creativity, and Psychopathology." (Commentary on "Creativity and Psychopathology" by Hans J. Eysenck.) *Psychological Inquiry,* 1993a, *4,* 212–217.

Richards, R. "Seeing Beyond: Issues of Creative Awareness and Social Responsibility." *Creativity Research Journal,* 1993b, *6,* 165–183.

Richards, R. "Creativity and Bipolar Mood Swings: Why the Association?" In M. P. Shaw and M. A. Runco (eds.), *Creativity and Affect.* Norwood, N.J.: Ablex, 1994.

Richards, R. "Does the Lone Genius Ride Again?: Creativity, Chaos, and Community." *Journal of Humanistic Psychology,* in press a, *36* (2).

Richards, R. "Everyday Creativity and the Arts." In A. Montuori and R. Purser (eds.), *Social Creativity: Prospects and Possibilities,* Vol. 3. Cresskill, N.J.: Hampton Press, in press b.

Richards, R. "When Illness Yields Creativity." In M. A. Runco and R. Richards (eds.), *Eminent Creativity, Everyday Creativity, and Health.* Norwood, N.J.: Ablex, in press c.

Richards, R., and Kinney, D. "Mood Swings and Creativity." *Creativity Research Journal,* 1990, *3,* 203–218.

Richards, R., Kinney, D., Daniels, H., and Linkins, K. "Everyday Creativity and Bipolar and Unipolar Affective Disorder: Preliminary Study of Personal and Family History." *European Psychiatry,* 1992, *7,* 49–52.

Richards, R., and others. "Creativity in Manic-Depressives, Cyclothymes, Their Normal Relatives, and Control Subjects." *Journal of Abnormal Psychology,* 1988, *97,* 281–288.

Runco, M. A., Johnson, D. J., and Bear, P. K. "Parents' and Teachers' Implicit Theories of Children's Creativity." *Child Study Journal,* 1993, *23,* 91–113.

Runco, M. A., and Okuda, S. M. "Reaching Creatively Gifted Children Through Their Learning Styles." In R. M. Milgram and R. Dunn (eds.), *Teaching the Gifted and Talented Through Their Learning Styles.* New York: Praeger, in press.

Runco, M. A., and Shaw, M. P. "Conclusions Concerning Creativity and Affect." In M. P. Shaw and M. A. Runco (eds.), *Creativity and Affect.* Norwood, N.J.: Ablex, 1994.

Russ, S. W. *Affect and Creativity: The Role of Affect and Play in the Creative Process.* Hillsdale, N.J.: Erlbaum, 1993.

Scales, B., Almy, M., Nicolopoulou, A., and Ervin-Tripp, S. *Play and the Social Context of Development in Early Care and Education.* New York: Teachers College Press, 1991.

Schuldberg, D. "Giddiness and Honor Horror in the Creative Process." In M. P. Shaw and M. A. Runco (eds.), *Creativity and Affect.* Norwood, N.J.: Ablex, 1994.

Shedler, J., Mayman, M., and Manis, M. "The Illusion of Mental Health." *American Psychologist,* 1993, *48,* 1117–1131.

Shenton, M. E., and others. "Thought Disorder in the Relatives of Psychotic Patients." *Archives of General Psychiatry,* 1989, *46,* 897–901.

Skarda, C., and Freeman, W. J. "How Brains Make Chaos in Order to Make Sense of the World." *Behavioral and Brain Sciences,* 1987, *10,* 161–173.

Smolucha, F. "A Reconstruction of Vygotsky's Theory of Creativity." *Creativity Research Journal,* 1992a, *5,* 49–67.

Smolucha, F. "The Relevance of Vygotsky's Theory of Creative Imagination for Contemporary Research on Play." *Creativity Research Journal,* 1992b, *5,* 69–76.

Solovay, M. D., and others. "Scoring Manual for the Thought Disorder Index (Revised Version)." *Schizophrenia Bulletin,* 1986, *12,* 483–496.

Tooby, J., and DeVore, I. "The Reconstruction of Hominid Behavioral Evolution Through Strategic Modeling." In W. G. Kinzey (ed.), *The Evolution of Human Behavior: Primate Models.* Albany: State University of New York Press, 1987.

Torrance, E. P., and Myers, R. E. *Creative Teaching and Learning.* New York: Dodd Mead, 1972.

Van Hoorn, J., Nourot, P., Scales, B., and Alward, K. *Play at the Center of the Curriculum.* New York: Macmillan, 1993.

Vygotsky, L. S. *Thought and Language.* Cambridge, Mass.: MIT Press, 1986.

Wallach, M. A. "Creativity." In P. H. Musses (eds.), *Carmichael's Manual of Child Psychology,* Vol. 1. New York: Wiley, 1970.

Westby, E. L., and Dawson, V. L. "Creativity: Asset or Burden in the Classroom?" *Creativity Research Journal,* 1995, *8,* 1–10.

Wilson, D. "Evolutionary Epidemiology." *Acta Biotheoretica,* 1992, *40.*

Wilson, E. O. *The Diversity of Life.* New York: Norton, 1992.

Wilson, E. O. "Is Humanity Suicidal?" *New York Times Magazine,* May 20, 1993, pp. 24–29.

RUTH RICHARDS is professor of psychology at Saybrook Institute; associate clinical professor of psychiatry at University of California, San Francisco; research affiliate at McLean Hospital; and assistant clinical professor of psychiatry at Harvard Medical School.

This chapter discusses important issues and needed research on creativity and development.

Creativity and Development: Recommendations

Mark A. Runco

A large number of issues are available to developmentalists interested in creativity. Many are covered in this volume; some are not. In this brief conclusion I highlight several of the other important issues and some of the more useful research on each. These citations are intended to complement those presented elsewhere in this volume. This conclusion starts with research on individuals within particular age groups, and then moves on to longitudinal research, research on developmental processes, and finally determinants of development, both extrinsic (for example, the family) and intrinsic (for example, learning).

Cross-Sectional and Longitudinal Research

Developmental research on creativity often focuses on a particular age, stage, or period. As such, this research makes the same kinds of contributions and uses the same assumptions as cross-sectional research conducted on other aspects of development. It does provide a useful picture of a particular group at a particular time. Smith has a series of papers on children, adolescents, and adults—including late adulthood (Smith and Carlsson, 1990). He suggests that creativity first appears in adolescence. Rothenberg (1990) also focuses on adolescence, but he admits that "if creativity is considered a general aspect of growth, it certainly would begin in childhood" (p. 417).

Developmental changes in creativity during adulthood are gaining more attention, and a more optimistic picture of late adulthood seems to be emerging. Lindauer (1992, 1993), Cohen-Shalev (1989), and Arnheim (1990), for example, see changes they called *old age style*. Smith's work can again be cited; he too found important developmental changes in late adulthood (Smith and Van der Meer, 1990).

New Directions for Child Development, no. 72, Summer 1996 © Jossey-Bass Publishers

Albert drew on his longitudinal research of exceptionally gifted children for his contribution to this volume. Additional details from that investigation are available in Albert (in press). Other longitudinal work on creativity has been conducted and reported by Milgram (in press), Harrington (in press), and Helson (in press).

Trends and Processes

Developmental trends have also been studied. This is a valuable line of work, especially for individuals interested in the processes that underlie development.

The research on developmental trends was recently reviewed by Runco and Charles (in press). They found continuities and discontinuities through-out the life span, and they acknowledged the possibility of uneven or asyn-chronous development. This conclusion is particularly applicable to creativity, given its widely accepted syndrome-complex definition. Certain traits and tal-ents within the complex can develop at one rate, while other traits and tal-ents, also in the complex, develop at different rates. Incidentally, the notion of uneven development apparently has a fairly long history: Hollingworth (1942) had something to say about it in her classic work published over fifty years ago.

The work of Smith (Smith and Carlsson, 1990) and Rothenberg (1990) can again be cited, for they viewed creativity as process. Smith, for example, relies on the *percept-genesis* technique, which is intended to uncover the basic cognitive and emotional processes that underlie creative thinking. As noted, Smith concluded that children are not truly creative, and that creativity first appears in adolescence. Rothenberg describes two processes used by individ-uals when creatively integrating more than one image or possibility: janusian and homospatial processes. Rothenberg describes how the variegated emo-tional needs of adolescents lead to a variegated cognition, which in turn allows for synthesis, integration, and creative insight.

Determinants of Development

Recommendations can also be given for research that focused on *determinants of development*. Albert (in press) can be cited here as well, especially for his work on procedural familial variables and parental personality as contributors to development of talent. Runco has described the relevance of structural famil-ial variables, including birth order, family size, and interval between or among siblings (Gaynor and Runco, 1992; Runco and Bahleda, 1987). No doubt addi-tional research on the family background of creativity should be conducted, especially because some dramatic changes in the family demographics of the United States have taken place in the past ten or twenty years.

Numerous developmental optima should be appreciated in the research on determinants of creativity. Runco and Gaynor (1993) identified several dozen optima for creativity, some in cognitive processes, some in family interactions, some in education, and so on (also see Runco and Sakamoto, 1996). More research should probably hypothesize optima instead of testing simple linear relationships.

Finally, there are intrinsic processes that influence the development of creativity. Learning can contribute to development, for example, as can maturational processes. Epstein (in press) and Runco (1993) presented views of the former, and Gardner (1982) the latter. Research using the Piagetian view, which is in many ways an interactionist one (that is, experience and maturation), was discussed in this volume by Richards and Runco, and discussed elsewhere by Gruber (in press), Levine (1984), and Runco (1993). Like Russ in this volume, Ayman-Nolley (1992), Smolucha (1992), and Daugherty (1993) have applied Vygotsky's theory to creativity. Several of these authors present theories of creativity and play.

It is probably apparent from the breadth of topics and approaches on this list that developmental research on creativity is quite common. This may be because it has special significance for our understanding of creativity. Indeed, creativity contributes to development, and it is influenced by other developmental processes. It is in some ways inextricable from development, just as it is inextricable from human nature. It may sound like a cliché, but it is nonetheless true that to be creative is to be human and to be open to development.

References

Albert, R. S. "Identity, Experiences, and Career Choice Among Exceptionally Gifted Boys." In M. A. Runco and R. S. Albert (eds.), *Theories of Creativity*. (Rev. ed.) Cresskill, N.J.: Hampton Press, in press.

Arnheim, R. "On the Late Style." In M. Perlmutter (ed.), *Late Life Potential*. Washington, D.C.: Gerontological Society of America, 1990.

Ayman-Nolley, S. "Vygotsky's Perspective on the Development of Imagination and Creativity." *Creativity Research Journal*, 1992, 5, 77–85.

Cohen-Shalev, A. "Old Age Style: Developmental Changes in Creative Production from a Life-Span Perspective." *Journal of Aging Studies*, 1989, 3, 21–37.

Daugherty, M. "Creativity and Private Speech." *Creativity Research Journal*, 1993, 6, 287–296.

Epstein, R. "Generativity Theory and Creativity." In M. A. Runco and R. S. Albert (eds.), *Theories of Creativity*. (Rev. ed.) Cresskill, N.J.: Hampton Press, in press.

Gardner, H. *Art, Mind, and Brain*. New York: Basic Books, 1982.

Gaynor, J.L.R., and Runco, M. A. "Family Size, Birth Order, Age-Interval, and the Creativity of Children." *Journal of Creative Behavior*, 1992, 26, 108–118.

Gruber, H. E. "The Life Space of a Scientist: The Visionary Function and Other Aspects of Jean Piaget's Thinking." *Creativity Research Journal*, in press.

Harrington, D. M. "The Ecology of Human Creativity: A Psychological Perspective." In M. A. Runco and R. S. Albert (eds.), *Theories of Creativity*. (Rev. ed.) Cresskill, N.J.: Hampton Press, in press.

Helson, R. "In Search of the Creative Personality." *Creativity Research Journal*, in press.

Hollingworth, R. *Children Above 180 IQ*. Yonkers-on-Hudson, N.Y.: World Books, 1942.

Levine, S. H. "A Critique of the Piagetian Presuppositions of the Role of Play in Human Development and a Suggested Alternative: Metaphoric Logic Which Organizes the Play Experience Is the Foundation for Rational Creativity." *Journal of Creative Behavior*, 1984, 18, 90–108.

Lindauer, M. S. "Creativity in Aging Artists: Contributions from the Humanities to the Psychology of Old Age." *Creativity Research Journal*, 1992, *5*, 211–231.

Lindauer, M. S. "The Span of Creativity Among Long-Lived Historical Artists." *Creativity Research Journal*, 1993, *6*, 221–239.

Milgram, R. M. "Creativity: An Idea Whose Time Has Come and Gone?" In M. A. Runco and R. S. Albert (eds.), *Theories of Creativity*. (Rev. ed.) Cresskill, N.J.: Hampton Press, in press.

Rothenberg, A. "Creativity in Adolescence." *Psychoanalytic Clinics of North America*, 1990, *13*, 415–434.

Runco, M. A. "Operant Theories of Insight, Originality, and Creativity." *American Behavioral Scientist*, 1993, *37*, 59–74.

Runco, M. A., and Bahleda, M. D. "Birth Order and Divergent Thinking." *Journal of Genetic Psychology*, 1987, *148*, 119–125.

Runco, M. A., and Charles, R. "Developmental Trends in Creative Potential and Creative Performance." In M. A. Runco (ed.), *Creativity Research Handbook*, Vol. 1. Cresskill, N.J.: Hampton Press, in press.

Runco, M. A., and Gaynor, J.L.R. "Creativity as Optimal Development." In J. Brzezinski, S. DiNuovo, T. Marek, and T. Maruszewski (eds.), *Creativity and Consciousness: Philosophical and Psychological Dimensions*. Amsterdam: Rodopi, 1993.

Runco, M. A., and Sakamoto, S. O. "Optimization as a Guiding Principle in Research on Creative Problem Solving." In T. Helstrup, G. Kaufmann, and K. H. Teigen (eds.), *Problem Solving and Cognitive Processes: Essays in Honor of Kjell Raaheim*. London: Kingsley, 1996.

Smith, G.J.W., and Carlsson, I. M. *The Creative Process: A Functional Model Based on Empirical Studies from Early Childhood to Middle Age*. Madison, Conn.: International Universities Press, 1990.

Smith, G.J.W., and van der Meer, G. "Creativity in Old Age." *Creativity Research Journal*, 1990, *3*, 249–264.

Smolucha, F. "The Relevance of Vygotsky's Theory of Creative Imagination for Contemporary Research on Play." *Creativity Research Journal*, 1992, *5*, 69–76.

MARK A. RUNCO is professor of child development at California State University, Fullerton.

Name Index

SUBJECT INDEX

Abnormality: creativity and, 69, 73. *See also* Psychiatric illness

Accommodation, 74–75

Adaptation: assimilation/accommodation and, 74; creativity and, 7, 13, 45, 69; evolutionary view and, 23; paradox of, 7; play and, 68, 74; transformation and, 4

Aesthetic emotion, 15

Affect: cognition and, 19; creative state and, 23, 77; divergent thinking and, 37–38; model of, and creativity, 31–34; play and, 34–40

Affect in Play Scale (APS), 37–39

Affective processes, 32–34, 37; access to affect-laden states, 32, 35–37; affective pleasure in challenge/problem solving, 34; cognitive integration of affective material, 34, 37; openness to affect states, 34, 37

Analytic thinking, 79

Assimilation, 74–75

Chaos theory: creativity and, 71–72, 82; edge-of-chaos phenomenon and, 71; emergent structures and, 71; human physiology and, 72

Chaotic amplification, 70–71

Childhood creativity: Affect in Play Scale and, 38–40; age factor in, 50; analytic/inferential thinking and, 79–80; anxiety and, 46, 50; combinatory imagination and, 36; conflict and, 68; convention-bound environment and, 51–52; creation of transitional objects and, 46–47; creative orientation and, 44; dead period of, 51; developmental continuity of, 58–62, 65; developmental discontinuity of, 9, 43, 45; differences in, 62–65; different nature of, 44; diversity and, 68; education and, 44; ego defenses and, 50–51; enterprise of, 60–61; experiential gaps and, 43, 47–48; facilitating, 40, 80–81, 83; family influence and, 44; first occurrence of, 24; habituation and, 81–82; imagination and, 78; impediments to, 51–52;

knowledge organization and, 60–61; love of activity and, 60–61; noncognitive variables/experiences and, 44; novelty/curiosity and, 47–48; observations on, 43–45; origins of, 44; parent loss/separation and, 46; parent-child experience and, 45–46; pathologization of, 81; perseverance and, 62; play and, 34–40; predictiveness of, 31; primary process thinking and, 35–36, 77; processes in, 31–34; puberty and, 44–45, 48–49; self-discipline and, 67; social/communicative aspects of, 74; teachability of, 52; teachers' valuation of, 68–69

Children: art of, 8; as cognitive aliens, 8; conceptual development of, 75; divergent thinking in, 38–40; happiness of, 68; innovation and, 7; intentionality and, 17; magical thinking of, 67–68. *See also* Childhood creativity

Cognition: affect and, 19; analytic/inferential thinking and, 79–80; creative problem solving, 32; divergent thinking and, 32, 36–40, 67; metacognition and, 19, 80; primary process thinking and, 35–36, 77. *See also* Cognitive development; Complexes, thinking in; Creative thinking

Cognitive development: adaptation and, 74; analytic/inferential thinking and, 79–80; assimilation/accommodation and, 74–75; cognitive threshold and, 62; curiosity and, 48; denial and, 48–49; divergent thinking and, 32, 36–40, 67; ego defenses and, 49–51; exploration and, 48; historical records of, 62; integrating modes of thought and, 77–78; preconcepts and, 75; primary process thinking and, 35–36, 77; primitive conceptual modes and, 75–79; puberty and, 44–45, 48–49; syncretic conglomerations and, 75–76; thinking in complexes and, 75–76; transformational abilities and, 32. *See also* Complexes, thinking in; Development; Primitive conceptual modes/process

ORDERING INFORMATION

NEW DIRECTIONS FOR CHILD DEVELOPMENT is a series of paperback books that presents the latest research findings on all aspects of children's psychological development, including their cognitive, social, moral, and emotional growth. Books in the series are published quarterly in Fall, Winter, Spring, and Summer and are available for purchase by subscription and individually.

SUBSCRIPTIONS for 1996 cost $59.00 for individuals (a savings of 22 percent over single-copy prices) and $87.00 for institutions, agencies, and libraries. Standing orders are accepted. New York residents, add local sales tax for subscriptions. (For subscriptions outside the United States, add $7.00 for shipping via surface mail or $25.00 for air mail. Orders *must be prepaid* in U.S. dollars by check drawn on a U.S. bank or charged to VISA, MasterCard, or American Express.)

SINGLE COPIES cost $19.00 plus shipping (see below) when payment accompanies order. California, New Jersey, New York, and Washington, D.C., residents, please include appropriate sales tax. Canadian residents, add GST and any local taxes. Billed orders will be charged shipping and handling. No billed shipments to post office boxes. (Orders from outside the United States *must be prepaid* in U.S. dollars by check drawn on a U.S. bank or charged to VISA, MasterCard, or American Express.)

SHIPPING (SINGLE COPIES ONLY): one issue, add $5.00; two issues, add $6.00; three issues, add $7.00; four to five issues, add $8.00; six to seven issues, add $9.00; eight or more issues, add $12.00.

DISCOUNTS FOR QUANTITY ORDERS are available. Please write to the address below for information.

ALL ORDERS must include either the name of an individual or an official purchase order number. Please submit your order as follows:
   Subscriptions: specify series and year subscription is to begin
   Single copies: include individual title code (such as CD59)

MAIL ALL ORDERS TO:
   Jossey-Bass Publishers
   350 Sansome Street
   San Francisco, California 94104-1342

FOR SUBSCRIPTION SALES OUTSIDE OF THE UNITED STATES, contact any international subscription agency or Jossey-Bass directly.

OTHER TITLES AVAILABLE IN THE
NEW DIRECTIONS FOR CHILD DEVELOPMENT SERIES
William Damon, Editor-in-Chief